PETER'S BOAT

Renewing the Vitality of Burned-Out Church Workers

BILL KEMP

DISCIPLESHIP RESOURCES

P O BOX 340003 • NASHVILLE, TN 37203-0003
www.discipleshipresources.org

Cover design by Christa Schoenbrodt.

Library of Congress Cataloging-in-Publication Data

Kemp, Bill, 1954-
  Ezekiel's bones : rekindling your congregation's spiritual passion /
Bill Kemp.
     p. cm.
  ISBN 978-0-88177-499-3
  I. Christian leadership. I. Title.
  BV652.1.K46 2007
  269—dc22

                            2007007524

Contents

Chapter Three: The Truth about Work Addiction 73

Chapter Four: Boundaries and Burnout 91

Preface

Burnout is a common condition in today's world:

- there are too few hours in the day;
- there are too few dollars in the paycheck;
- there are too many expectations left to be met;
- there is too much running around and doing what we don't enjoy doing;
- we have all forgotten what first motivated us to take on all these things.

Burnout is common no matter where one works or volunteers today.

Burnout is also a church problem:

- there are too few hours to prepare for worship and those who lead often don't communicate the gospel with freshness and joy;
- there is too little in the church budget to compensate the pastor and staff;
- there are too many expectations placed on both the clergy and lay leadership;

- there are too many volunteers doing what they aren't equipped or interested in doing;
- those who once were creative dreamers have now become negative, inflexible, tradition-bound, and territorial as they go about their tasks;
- we have all forgotten what first led us to give so much of our lives to this very human institution we call our church.

And when we are burned-out we become:

- overly anxious;
- easily angered;
- overwhelmed;
- less confident in our abilities.

We may feel:

- depressed;
- under appreciated;
- irritable;
- emotionally detached or shut-down;
- socially cut-off;
- tempted to engage in addictive or foolish behavior.

We may experience:

- insomnia;
- physical ailments, such as stomach problems, headaches, neck strain, back problems, etc.;
- chronic conditions, such as weight gain (or loss), sexual dysfunction, high blood pressure, asthma and allergies, panic and phobic disorders, etc.

Further, when leaders of congregations or denominational officials become convinced that there just are not enough resources or people to keep the church going, a scarcity mentality sets in that seeks to preserve institutions and traditions ahead of people and healthy spiritual relationships. These individuals and committees may be oblivious to how their attitude compromises the health of those who work in the church. Burnout at this point moves from being an individual concern to being a communal death spiral that envelops the whole organization.

This book will offer you hope and practical solutions. To the burned-out, it is a guide back to vitality. For church staff, it provides a blueprint for healthy policies and attitudes. These will help protect your key people from burnout. Some congregations have habits and customs that their volunteers and staff people to grow weary and drop out. This book offers both the plan for change and the incentive to make it work. Burnout is not inevitable. It is both preventable and curable.

> Even youths grow tired and weary, and young men
>   stumble and fall;
> but those who hope in the Lord will renew their
>   strength.

> They will soar on wings like eagles;
> they will run and not grow weary, they will walk and
>   not be faint (Isaiah 40:30-31).

Introduction: "What Is Burnout?"

"Let us not become weary in doing good . . ."

Galatians 6:9a

Do you remember when church was fun? Has it become just another rat race for you? I am not saying you no longer believe in the importance of the work of the church, but if your Christian service no longer rewards you, you may be experiencing burnout. This book will help you understand where the joy went and why so many people are becoming weary of well-doing today.

Think about the rat running a maze in a lab. The scientist can get this animal to learn a new behavior by rewarding it with chunks of cheese scattered throughout the maze. Once the lab rat has learned the behavior, the rewards can be spaced out and eventually stopped altogether. The poor creature will keep running the maze and doing its tricks, over and over, even though it gets nothing for its works. Given the proper behavior modification, the rat will keep running its maze until it starves. Human beings are subject to the same laws of behavior modification and the manipulation of diminishing rewards. One sees the same process in how religious cults recruit new people. In the church, some of us have become over-committed, work-addicted, and trapped in dependent relationships because we enjoy the initial rush of people saying how

9

much they appreciate our efforts. Driven by the satisfaction of doing "the right thing," we enter these mazes that do not offer us places to consider our personal needs or reflect on what appropriate limits we should place on our behavior.

Like a lobster caught in a trap, life presents us with boxes that are easy to get into and hard to exit. These traps take many forms. It may be a relationship with one other person where we find ourselves always giving and never receiving. It may be an investment in a sure-fire stock or in some Florida swampland. It may be a job, either in the secular world or in the church. It may be a volunteer experience or a recreational activity where the commitment expected from each participant keeps getting raised higher and higher. Eventually, the energy required of us outweighs any joy we experience in the activity. Any investment, whether it is a financial deal, a job, a church, or a club, can reach the point where it is no longer fun. The difference between humans and the laboratory animals is that the rats never lose hope in their reward. We eventually come to a point of awareness where our conscious mind admits that this situation is no longer worth our investment. At that point, we will enter a state of being "of two minds." Part of us still wants to keep running the maze, while another part—the rational, inner voice—urges us to cut our losses and drop out. This state of being of two minds is inherently exhausting. In fact, we cannot be content as long as our heart (or will) is divided in this way. Jesus alludes to this in Matthew 6:22-24a:

> The eye is the lamp of the body. If your eyes are good, your whole body will be full of light.
>
> But if your eyes are bad, your whole body will be full of darkness. If then the light within you is darkness, how great is that darkness! "No one can serve two masters. Either he will hate the one and love the other, or he will be devoted to the one and despise the other . . .

Jesus begins by noting how the eyes bring light into our souls by their ability to focus on one thing, and then moves on to the frank statement that no one can serve two masters. One cannot be of two minds for long. Just as one cannot serve God and money, it also follows that one cannot be both aware of diminishing returns of ones work and fully function as a healthy human being. When one becomes aware that things are not what one hopes them to be, it feels like the candle of one's ideals has been blown out. **Burnout is the state of running a maze without reward, and knowing it.**

The symptoms of burnout are similar to that of physical exhaustion. One feels tired, weak, unmotivated, and unwilling to think beyond the next step or task. But since burnout is a psychological state, it can lead to some or all of the following:

- depression;

- anger;

- loss of self-confidence;

- cynicism about the motives of others;

- loss of the ability to see "the big picture;"

- negative attitude about ones career;

- lack of creativity;

- low enthusiasm about new things and the future.

Further, the stress of exhaustion can generate or aggravate a variety of psychosomatic illnesses, such as weight gain (or loss), sexual dysfunction, stomach problems, headaches, neck strain, back problems, high blood pressure, etc. Please note that in saying that a condition may be psychosomatic I am not saying that it is in anyway less real or may not have arisen from a pre-existing physical defect. The mind and body and soul are intimately interrelated and the energy required to keep running without reward must come from somewhere. What the soul commits us to the body and the mind must be willing to pay for.

Remember when you first became involved in church. What were the rewards you received for participating in congregational life? Did you find that the weekly act of worship nurtured a deep connection between your soul and the holy otherness of God? Did you enter your workweek feeling renewed and centered, prepared to face life's difficulties? Were there aspects of the church's teachings and biblical doctrines that you found helpful in sorting out the nature of human existence and what lays beyond the grave? Recall the first time someone asked you to do a job in the church. Did the rewards of doing something that made a difference as a volunteer excite you? Could you sense that the Holy Spirit had indeed equipped you to do some valuable things through this fellowship of Christians? And finally, do you remember how much you enjoyed the extended circle of new relationships with other people that your first involvement in the church provided? The church is unique in the way it forms small, intimate fellowship circles where people can connect with others facing similar life situations. It also provides large group interactions that are intergenerational and provide a foretaste of the diversity that will mark heaven. Many of us discovered our spouses as well as established our life-long friendships through participating in church related activities.

While serving God through our church work is exciting at first, most of us begin to sense that the personal rewards for our ministry are becoming more and more spaced out. We experience a conflict or two in the church setting that sobers our enthusiasm and trust of our congregation as a place that nurtures loving relationships. People move, become divorced or inactive, or pass on, and it saddens us because we no longer receive the rewards of a rich fellowship life. We also gradually become less enamored by the importance of what we do for the good of the kingdom of God. So much of what we do in the church seems trivial and trite. The meetings we attend remind us of the ancient Greek myth of Sisyphus, where a man was condemned to push the same rock up a steep hill, only to have it roll back down time and time again. Moreover, the church's rich theological rewards and answers to life's most intriguing questions become forgotten in the midst of financial concerns over paying the church's bills. The more we become involved in leadership, the more aware we become of the constant crisis surrounding the lack of volunteers to do the church's programs. Filling in for those who don't show up or who under perform disturbs our spiritual rhythm.

Somewhere, we go from being Mary at the feet of Jesus, to being Martha in the kitchen washing the pots and pans.

Finally, and most importantly, worship no longer satisfies our souls even though we may from time to time feel as though it has gone well. Our focus shifts to the quality and perfectibility of the worship hour, rather than the gift of God who is present with us. For many of us, our responsibilities for things being done right during the church's most hectic hour of the week affects our ability to find the weekly reward that our souls need to go on. Pulpit ministry draws many clergy because it provides us with an opportunity to use our gift for creative communication. But the church craves consistency, and soon we find that other emergencies squeeze out the time we need for innovation. We learn to recycle old sermons and make full use of canned pulpit digests rather than engage in the joyful and soul satisfying work of exploring the biblical text for ourselves. Burnout is not so much related to the hours of time spent in the tasks of church work. It is a reflection of the rarity of the rewards we first found when we became involved with those tasks.

Blaming the Church

To admit that the church can cause burnout in committed persons puts the church in the same bad company as those who run lab rats through mazes, sell pyramid schemes, abuse their employees, and manipulate the vulnerable. I am willing to make that accusation while still believing that the church is of God, will be used by the Lord to save the world, and will continue to be a great source of earthly joy for its members. The simple truth is that the church is a human institution built upon a divine foundation. To labor in the church is to deal with a strange mixture of the holy and the profane. I am convinced that God lovingly provides consistent and sustained rewards for each of us as we sacrifice for the church. All of us, however, are tempted by rewards that are not good for us and that are poor substitutes of God's loving gifts. Each church is a complex human system. Many congregations unwittingly adopt manipulative strategies and form a leadership culture that provides diminishing rewards for those who run the race of faith. Often, the church is no more trustworthy than the drug dealer or the loan shark. These are harsh words, but as we explore in future chapters the failure of many clergy to take weekly Sabbath days, the propensity of finance committees to be utterly life draining, and the cruelty of the misplacement of laity into church work that they are not gifted to do, we will begin to see how far many congregations stray from their divine foundation. Paul writes:

> . . . each one should be careful how he builds. For no one can lay any foundation other than the one already laid, which is Jesus Christ. If any man builds on this foundation using gold, silver, costly stones, wood, hay or straw, his work will be shown for what it is, because the Day will bring it to light. It will be revealed with fire, and the fire will test the quality of each man's work. If what he has built survives, he will receive his reward. If it is burned up, he will suffer loss; he himself will be saved, but only as one escaping through the flames. Don't you know that you yourselves are God's temple and that God's Spirit lives in you? (First Corinthians 3:10b-16).

When we suffer burnout in our church work, it is as if a spark has ignited dry tinder. All the things we have come to love about the church are now at risk. Our burnout threatens relationships, both with those who we have been trying to please as well as with those we have been trying to minister to. For those who the church employs, burnout threatens both our ability to perform our jobs and our very livelihood. For each of us, no matter what role we play in the church, the fire of burnout threatens the very way we perceive our faith. If burnout consumes our work in the church, were we ever really Christians? No wonder our first reaction is to run around trying to put the fire out. We deny, both to ourselves and to others, that we have become of two minds about the rewards of Christian service. In our quest to find water for the flames, we make poor compromises that may dowse the initial fire but leave us more vulnerable in the future. For example, we may duck out of an obligation to perform some task this week by making greater promises to be available later. Pastors who have become burned-out will skip their weekly Sabbath to attend workshops that they hope will teach them how to restore the vitality of their ministry. Our ears become more attuned to every promise of a quick fix, and we follow these leads without pausing to ascertain their viability. The state of knowing that we are burned-out, but not wanting to admit it to ourselves, is exhausting physically, mentally, and emotionally.

Each time the symptoms of burnout flare up in one of a congregation's respected leaders, it is like a fire has been discovered in the relational framework of the church. Those who know that this leader is exhausted and ready to resign or is acting with uncharacteristic edginess, want to keep this a secret for fear that other people will find out and question their own commitment to the organization. In congregations that have largely done their recruitment into church offices by using the wood, hay, and straw of guilt, manipulation, and unfulfilled promises, there is always the danger that the spark of one person's burnout may lead to desertion in mass. These congregations develop highly drilled fire brigades. This work of constantly putting out fires not only exhausts the leadership, it acts to distract the church from its purpose of making disciples. Further, I have found that congregations who are highly invested in maintaining an unhealthy work culture often have in their history a hidden secret, an incidence in which a leader has betrayed their trust by some misconduct. Because these congregations have failed to undergo the healing process that they need to deal with their misfortune, they bind all their leadership to unreasonable expectations. Like the other books of this leadership series, this book will talk about burnout as a systemic problem with a cure that involves making broad changes to a congregation's culture and daily behavior.

What Paul helps us to see by speaking apocalyptically in the above passage, is that individual cases of burnout are but preludes to that day when the Lord will come and test what each congregation has built. That which is not up to code will not survive. Maintaining systems that burn people out is both unproductive in the short run and costly on the Day of Judgment. Part of what it means to be a disciple of Jesus Christ is to develop for oneself a spiritual refreshment routine that allows one to be healthy and grow as a well-rounded person throughout ones life. Congregations are unlikely to be about their primary task of making disciples if they are expecting their leadership to sacrifice their own emotional, spiritual, and physical health for the cause. Clergy need to model self-care before their congregations. Laity should expect healthy work conditions to be in place for both their paid employees and for the church's volunteers. Further, the aspects of the church's life that will survive on the Day of Judgment—the church's faith, hope, and charity towards all—must be protected and kept pure from both the neurotic expectations that we place on ourselves as well as the manipulative guilt we sometimes thrust upon others.

Therefore, this is a book for everyone in the church. It will deal with the following four primary causes of burnout in church work:

- perfectionism;

- concerns about self-image (sometimes called "codependency");

- work addiction;

- overload (failure to set boundaries).

The above factors also combine with today's diminishing church financial resources to accelerate burnout's flame. Each factor is by itself sufficient to push us into madness. I rarely encounter a clergy or church staff person who does not have several of these ongoing issues smoldering away just below the level of his or her awareness, in addition to the current stressor he or she may be experiencing. An otherwise insignificant incident in his or her pastoral duties might bring to awareness the sense of diminishing rewards that will, in turn, kindle a forest fire of burnout. Laity may find themselves subject to one or two of the above in their church life, but then they compound their emotionally depleted state by bringing in factors from their secular employment and family situation.

People rarely realize that the cause, experience, and treatment of burnout are the same whether one is clergy or lay.

Throughout this book, I will intentionally address the concerns of volunteers, paid staff, and clergy. Further, leaders of congregations, particularly small ones, often speak of burnout as one of their most urgent communal problems. They say, "We have too few people doing too many jobs. Unless we do something, we all are going to become too tired to continue." This self-perception, that their church is a place of too many burdens and too few rewards, leads to reluctance to invite others to join them in the joy of worship as well as to an unconscious desire to trick those who do attend into taking on as many jobs as they possibly can. This indicates that burnout is a systemic problem as well as a personal one. When a community of people feels that their own survival justifies the use of guilt and manipulation to get people to serve, burnout becomes a pervasive situation. Further, many congregations foster a system of values that makes self-care and honesty about ones limitations a taboo topic.

Biblically Burned-Out

In this introduction I have spoken of burnout as being the state of having two minds, that is, people burn out when they become aware that they are no longer being rewarded as they once were for their behavior, but they still obey the conditioned mind that tells them to stay with the rat race and show up for whatever church obligations they have agreed to. I must admit that this is not the standard definition, which tends to focus on symptoms such as exhaustion, cynicism, depression, and feelings of low self-worth and anger. I like the simplicity of the definition offered by Lynne M. Baab:

> Burnout is exhaustion caused by a chronic stress over-load coupled with too few effective coping strategies [*Beating Burnout in Congregations* by Lynne M. Baab (Alban Institute, 2003), 27].

As this book progresses, I will return to the mainstream of thought on this subject and add to my definition from what others are saying.

But for now, I will characterize burnout as an awakened state, that is, the people who say that they are burned-out actually know something about their own soul which others in the church may be too busy to realize.

I see this quality of being "awakened" dramatized in Jesus' story of the Prodigal son. As he journeys away from home, the young man is at first overjoyed with the sensual rewards of his independent lifestyle. But as the weeks roll by, the rewards of being a "prodigal" become infrequent until he receives less than he needs to feed himself. While he feeds the pigs with pea pods that he would love to have, he comes to a sudden state of clarity about his situation, expressed in the pivotal verse:

> "When he came to his senses, he said, 'How many of
> my father's hired men have food to spare, and here I am
> starving to death!'" (Luke 15:17).

His awareness involves both the present danger he was in as well as a willingness to no longer be driven by pride or shame down a pathway that lacked rewards. Burnout sometimes provides us with a wake-up call that we are frittering our health away by our work habits. We will say, "Look at what the stress of my church work is doing to me! I'm not sleeping well, I'm losing (or gaining) weight, I snap at people, and I am beginning to feel depressed to the point where I don't even want to go near the church." These symptoms increase until we recognize the pride, guilt, and manipulation that have kept us locked into patterns of perfectionism, work addiction, codependency, and over-commitment to our ministry.

Luke's gospel also tells the famous story of how Jesus reacted to his friend Martha when she complained about her sister Mary's unwillingness to help out in the kitchen. This story has such obvious implications for any discussion about burnout that I have found it helpful in diagnosing where people are in their Christian service. Before someone comes to a place of "awareness" about burnout, they often side with Martha and become angry at how Jesus behaves in this story. He seems to have no sympathy at all for the hard working Martha. They say, "Why doesn't Jesus tell Mary to help out? If it weren't for the Martha's of the world cooking the meals and doing the dishes, God's people would be hungry and homeless." It is only after we have begun to recover from burnout that we see the wisdom of Jesus' response. He gently rebukes her saying:

> "Martha, Martha, . . . you are worried and upset about many things, but only one thing is needed. Mary has chosen what is better, and it will not be taken away from her" (Luke 10:41-42).

I think Jesus earnestly hopes to help Martha reach a new level of self-understanding. I see him fully accepting the fact that she has become stressed out, but he is aware that the solution does not lie in a fairer distribution of work. The people who are on the way towards burnout always believe that all of their problems will be solved if everyone just pitches in and does their fair share. Jesus, however, knows that burnout is not rooted in the laziness of others. Its roots lie in our own willingness to take on the additional burdens of perfectionism (chapter one), work addiction (chapter three), and codependency (this term will be defined in chapter two). Jesus tells Martha that only one thing is needed in this situation. That "one thing" may refer to the spiritual and self-awareness that prevents Mary from sacrificing the hour at Jesus' feet to her sister's plans. Or, it could be that Jesus is pointing to the dozens of dishes that Martha has chosen to prepare, implying that maybe only one simple plate of cold cuts was needed. In either case, focusing on what the situation reasonably required of her would have freed Martha to enjoy Jesus' visit. Today, many church people cannot enjoy the hour of worship because their attitude about the many things they feel need to be done each Sunday morning distracts them from the weekly visit of our Lord into his house. Martha, like many of us, has driven off the narrow road of proper Christian service and allowed her perfectionism and work addiction to plow her into the ditch of despair. Not all of those who stuck in that rut find their way out. Many continue to muddle on, far from the joyful understanding of God's goodness, freedom, and grace that initially drew them to Jesus. Like the prodigal son, Martha and all those she represents desperately need to come to a state of awareness.

Types of Christian Workers

With this understanding we can easily determine that there are four kinds of Christians involved in church work today:

First, there are the healthy ones. These people maintain a healthy spirituality through their involvement in Christian service. They allow themselves time to sit at the Lord's feet, like Mary, and plan into their week worship and rest experiences that fulfill their need for Sabbath. Because they have a healthy attitude about their own salvation, they do not seek the approval of others or race around trying to achieve some mistaken notion of perfection. They have put boundaries around their commitments so that they don't become overwhelmed by work that doesn't line up with their gifts. They also don't have unrealistic expectations of their fellow Christians. When conflict occurs, they accept that even the church is a human institution marked by sin. Having said this, they look for God's grace rather than their own manipulations to solve the issue. They are life-long disciples who do not have to fear becoming burned-out.

Second, there are the dedicated lab rats. These are some of the best workers in the church, because they do not know how to say "no." They are already caught in the trap of diminishing spiritual returns from their church work in general and particularly as it relates to their participation in worship. No matter what their role is on Sunday morning, they are the ones who return home exhausted by their "day of rest." They run the maze endlessly because they have set no boundaries around what they will and will not do. Further, others easily manipulate them through guilt and by the myth that things in the church should somehow be perfect. They look to this human institution to provide all of their relational needs, often withholding love and nurturing time from their spouse and children in order to attend church functions. Because they have bought into this reward system of diminishing returns and random reinforcement, most of the joy and blessings that should accompany church life occurred in the past for them. For this reason, they are often tradition bound, fearful of change, and unwilling to take the risks that they and the church need to enter a new future. This past orientation, remembering where the cheese once was, keeps them running around propping up programs that ought to have been abandoned or turned over to fresh leadership. They are too busy to be aware, are unlikely to seek help from others or to read books such as this one, and so are trapped in the maze that will inevitably lead to burnout.

Third, there are the burned-out. These are people who have come to see the glimpses of how the current reality of their religious life varies from the expectations they had when they took on an active role in church leadership. They may be just allowing into their consciousness a sense of the problem, or they may be actively seeking alternatives and discussing their feelings with others. They often remain some of our best church workers because they do not want to abandon what they have given so much of their lives to support, but there is now an edge to their response when they are asked to do additional tasks. Because they are living in two minds, they may be exhausted, depressed, lack their former confidence in their abilities do things well, be cynical about the motives of others, lack the ability to see "the big picture," and have a negative attitude about new things and the future. Because they are becoming aware, however, they are less easily manipulated by guilt and are more realistic about what their church is able to do. They will become unwilling to play the game of brushing the interpersonal conflicts of the congregation under the rug, but will speak truthfully about the lack of love they see expressed around them. As their sense of awareness and inner wisdom grows, they will incorporate into their daily lives the prayer of the once over committed and addicted, which goes:

> God grant me the serenity
> to accept the things I cannot change;
> courage to change the things I can;
> and wisdom to know the difference
> (attributed to Reinhold Niebuhr).

Burnout, then, is a state of blessing far better to be in than that of the lab rat above, just as labor is a better state to be in than pregnancy. It is, however, also a state of danger. One cannot remain burned-out for long: either one will discover the pathway back to the healthy state of the first person above, or one will drop out, falling prey to the exhaustion, depression, cynicism, self-doubt, narrow mindedness, general negativism, and in order to survive, become an inactive church member. This book focuses on how to use the awareness that burnout brings to find one's way back to a healthy church life. It also will discuss some of the systemic changes congregations can do to encourage healthy Christian service and make the road of recovery easier for those who are burned-out.

The fourth and final state of church leaders is that of the terminally burned-out. These are the stillborn children of burnout's spiritual process. They remind us of Paul's words above to the church at Corinth. They have been through a fire and have found all of their religious involvements consumed by their awareness that church work is no longer rewarding. Some have nothing left to give, and depart Christian service holding on to their personal faith like refugees fleeing with only their clothes on their backs. Others become convinced that even their faith is dead. Even though I believe that God mercifully makes our salvation of much firmer stuff than we ever understand upon this earth, it is significant that so many of the terminally burned-out no longer express any hopes of heaven. I think each congregation will be held accountable for those whom they have pushed into this terminal state.

But there is also still hope, and if a congregation manages to win one back by expressing winsome grace and forbearance from laying on undue burdens to those who have become terminally burned-out, there should be a profound sense of joy. What I am proposing is that, in a society where many are burned-out in their secular lives, and many more have become burned-out in their church work, the church that practices compassionate concern for the health of its worshipers and teaches appropriate self-care for its leaders will become a true, twenty-first century, soul-saving station. As the old gospel song urges us, we must "rescue the perishing." Many of those who perish today are work addicted, dependency crazed, and terminally burned-out.

My Own Story

My father cashed in his stocks and retired at age forty-nine. Even to my naive high school eyes he looked seriously burned-out, and I made a mental note not to enter an occupation that would do that to a person. Yet, my father had worked in a science technology field that he loved. Making full use of the GI bill and the postwar expansion of this business, he had rapidly climbed the career ladder from a hands-on engineering entry position, to a design level job, to management, and then part ownership of a new start-up company. Barely into mid-life, however, he became disenchanted with this work. His engineering mind noted that the rewards of his labor, especially the intrinsic relational and soul-filling ones, were becoming more and more spaced out and may soon disappear. He departed his vocation at about the same time I felt my calling into ministry and was preparing to enter seminary. Neither of us had any interest in just working for a paycheck. We wanted our labor to be soul-fulfilling.

As I approached forty-nine, I experienced a series of life-changing events. Situations in my family relationships forced me to recognize that I had emotionally overly invested in the church and needed to spend more time at home. I came to the realization that being a "busy pastor" did not excuse my being unavailable to my wife and nearly grown children. Further, I found my own personal sense of identity had been eaten away by my 24/7 involvement in ministry. If I wasn't running off to a meeting or leading worship, I didn't know who I was. Taking advantage of a sabbatical leave funded by the Lilley Endowment, I began to read extensively the literature on burnout, codependence, and clergy stress, as well as reflect upon how congregations behave as complex social systems. This time off also served to awaken in me a love for writing. When I returned back to pastoral duties, I knew that much of my job description as the senior pastor of an urban church with staff lay outside my natural area of giftedness. I am not wired by God to handle employees or to attend endless meetings. The sabbatical had done much to restore my spiritual and emotional health, but it also had awakened in me a reluctance to return to the old rat race.

The month that ended my sabbatical also contained the tragic events of 9/11. The week I returned to parish duties I received word that my father had had a stroke, and for the next two weeks until his passing, I led the divided existence of working to catch up with things in my church on the east coast and wanting to be with my dying father in the west. In the midst of all this, I became aware that some of my key laity of the congregation had lost confidence in my ministry among them and questioned if I should return to lead that congregation. They wanted me either to come back, giving twice as much to the church to make up for lost time, or to move on. Unlike my pre-midlife self, I was now unwilling to respond to this pressure by diving further into work. I instead began to say "no" and to actively pursue what was in my self-interest and would further the health of my family. As the months went by, I prayerfully discerned a plan that would allow me to shift into my current ministry. This plan involved writing, consulting, and serving interim assignments. This has necessitated additional training and more work hours than my previous parish work, and a significant reduction in income. You would think that the increased travel, financial concerns, and work responsibilities would exacerbate the sense of being burned-out that I had in 2001, but now I feel much more committed to the church and spiritually alive than I have at any point in the previous twenty-five years. Burnout can lead to restored heath if we honor it as a spiritual process that leads us through awareness towards a different way of going about our Christian duties.

Five Stages of Burnout

I have been trying to redefine burnout as a state of awareness where we come to realize our own divided soul and learn that we are being rewarded only rarely for carrying the burden of emotional stress and spiritual neglect that we have committed ourselves to by our current way of serving the church. Besides being a process of increasing awareness, burnout is a learning situation for us as Christians. I believe that we come to experience burnout because we need to know something that we did not know before. The Holy Spirit is our teacher in this process.

Scott Peck in his book, *Denial of the Soul*, speaks about the five stages of grief that Dr. Elizabeth Kübler-Ross discovered in her studies of the terminally ill. Peck then goes on to make this important generalization:

> Although Dr. Külber-Ross didn't quite realize it at the time she wrote *On Death and Dying*, she had outlined stages that we go through anytime we make significant a psychospiritual growth step at any point during our lives [*Denial of the Soul: Spiritual and Medical Perspectives on Euthanasia and Mortality* by M. Scott Peck, M.D. (Harmony Books, NY 1997)].

Burnout is for us a place of "psycho-spiritual growth" and like the dying, we find ourselves engaged in denial, anger, bargaining, depression, and acceptance (but not always in that order) as we process the new learning that it thrusts upon us. Even though each person's spiritual journey is unique, Kübler-Ross's stages provide a helpful "you are here" type map for the burnout experience. Further, as I have done transitional consulting with congregations adjusting to trauma and leadership change, I have found these five stages provide a framework for understanding the overall social system of a church. Whenever a congregation is confronted about their tendency to cause their leaders to burnout, they will respond with these same five steps.

1) DENIAL

Burnout begins with our getting warnings from others, from our inner emotional voice, and sometimes from our own bodies about our condition. We, however, deny these warnings and refuse to use the word "burnout" to describe our state. We say, "Oh I am under a little bit of stress right now, but I know how to handle it." As burnout progresses, we become more emphatic in our denial of both the symptoms of our condition as well as of the fact that we are doing anything wrong by persisting in our current path. The stress that we are experiencing is a message to change course and do the reflective work that is good for our souls. We seek to manage stress by denying its pain and ability to do long-term damage to our relationships, bodies, and mental health. Further, when we don't move through denial and onto awareness, we establish a pattern of thinking that makes us vulnerable to the addiction process. Those who wish to remain in denial and be better able to "handle stress" often seek chemical solutions.

2) ANGER

The harder it is to maintain denial in the face of people who tell us that we need to take a break emotionally from that which concern us (such as chaotic thoughts, addictive cravings, depression, lack of concentration, insomnia) and from the physical symptoms of stress, the more we experience unexpected fits of anger. We snap back at the loved one who asks us to take a day off. We get angry at ourselves for missing an appointment or failing to be able to get the sleep we need. We carry a generalized anger against our body that refuses to keep up with the high-paced life we enjoyed as a younger person. We are like the man who was so enraged when he arrived at a destination late that he kicked the tires of his car, only to break his toe and have to spend the remainder of the day in the emergency room. This anger at our own failure to handle stress and maintain our denial in the face of what others and our bodies are saying to us will at some point become transformed into a different kind of anger. The anger of denial gives way to the anger of awareness. We wake up to realize that we are burned-out, and it has to be somebody's fault. We blame our boss, our spouse, our church council, our parents, and often, we blame ourselves most of all. While the anger of denial often can be covered by a sweet smile, the anger of awareness turns us from Dr. Jeckle to Mr. Hyde. As I noted in my own story above, we reach the point where we no longer know ourselves. I found myself saying, "Who is this person who is lashing out at my wife and congregants?"

3) BARGAINING

Bargaining is our attempt to have our cake and eat it too. We recognize that there is a problem, but we are not willing to admit that our burnout will take an entire reorganization of our lives to resolved it. Because we think our situation has been caused simply by taking on too much, we respond by dropping one or two items from our week's agenda. We fail to recognize that our souls are starving because the spiritual rewards we once experienced are no longer being provided. The classical example of bargaining is the workaholic who agrees to take a short vacation, thinking it will solve the symptoms of burnout she has been experiencing and get her nagging husband off her back. She attempts to squeeze all the rejuvenation she has been missing over the years into her five or six day holiday. Crash courses in relaxation rarely work. We come back making promises to spend more quality time with family members and to take better care of ourselves in the future. Our spouse takes a "I'll believe it when I see it" attitude. He or she knows we are only bargaining, we have not yet come to the place where we are willing to seriously invest in making our lives more livable.

The bargaining that is being done here is between the burned-out person and his or her symptoms. To reach resolution, we must look past our feelings of anger, overload, depression, and self-blame, and dig down to the root of our problem. We must work the process to the point where we come to understand the hidden nature of perfectionism, codependency, work addiction, and failure to form adequate boundaries. Rather than making a bargain with stress and making shallow promises, we need to make new agreements with our innermost selves and discover what makes our souls happy. To get through, we first have to do things that will seem to make the problem worse. We may have to take time out of our work schedule to attend therapy or have intentional retreat times. This will make our overload problem seem worse and force us to make serious choices for life-long health. Many people have discovered that before they can say no to what they need to say no to, they need to first go through a period of saying no to everything.

4) DEPRESSION

People often talk about their burnout as an exhaustion that lingers even when they have had enough rest and are away from the situations that cause stress in their church work. They feel dull and lifeless. Depression is the natural consequence of realizing that denial, anger, and bargaining has not solved the problem of one's burnout. Having made a human attempt at doing an end-run around the reality of one's burnout, one is left with the realization that the only way forward is to return back to the beginning and rebuild one's Christian service on a different foundation. Guilt and perfectionism has brought us this far, but now we have to return to our spiritual roots and begin again, just trusting in grace. Depression always accompanies this stage of burnout because we find ourselves mourning the old life of over-commitment and being the person everyone depends upon. As much as we might hate the rate race that has caused us to be burned-out, we still find ourselves sad about leaving it behind.

Having said this about depression as a step in the five-step (Kübler-Ross) grief process, it is important to say that depression is also a mental health concern. Whether depression occurs in the midst of burnout or in some other point in one's life, one may need to seek treatment for it. Nearly everyone experiences periods of depression when he or she feel sad for no reason, has a general loss of energy, or no longer experiences interest in activities that he or she once enjoyed. We pass through these moods and sometimes afterwards can reflect back and note how our mental state might have been related to some particular stress in our lives or might be the understandable feeling of deflation that occurs after completing a hard-worked project. Normal depression is brief and episodic. However, sustained or reoccurring depression needs treatment. Managing depression, whether through antidepressant medication or therapy (or better still, some combination of the two), compliments the process of burnout recovery. A person who is both seriously depressed and burned-out needs to work on both issues simultaneously. Congregations also need to free their leaders to seek psychological treatment, surrounding those who are engaged in therapy with respect and confidentiality.

5) ACCEPTANCE

Acceptance may not be the best word for the final step in the healing process of burnout, which is one of intentional resolution. As a learning experience, burnout leads us to accept certain things about ourselves, such as our human imperfections, need for rest, limitations, and most importantly, our dependence upon the grace of God. But this acceptance has to generate positive lifestyle changes. We need to form boundaries, learn how to say no, develop a healthy self-image, and seek spiritual rewards in the midst of our church work. This final state is not passive, but actively finds practical ways to implement our new learning.

God's Fuse Box

The word *burnout* always reminds me of the old fashion electrical fuse that melts under too much current and plunges the house into darkness at the most inconvenient time. We curse the failure of the fuse, just as we curse the experience of burnout in our church work. But when we experience a stress overload as Christians, no matter how devastating the symptoms of that burnout is, there is something vital about your soul that is being protected by this spiritual fuse. This book will not teach you how to put pennies into the emotional fuse box of your life or of your congregational system. I have learned too much from my own personal experience of burnout not to be willing to cheat the safety measures of God.

It is because I see burnout as a positive thing that this book will be different from other self-help books that attempt to teach us how to manage stress. Instead, I will first seek to provide language and promote clarity around the issues of church life that lead us to feel burned-out. Second, I will address the difficult issue of how we can remain leaders in the church while we struggle with the personal experiences that often accompany burnout. Third, I will provide support for those who want to go beyond bargaining with stress and implement changes in the church and in their own lifestyle that address the lessons of burnout. Finally, I will provide scriptural guidance for those leaders who wish to make their congregation a healthier place and improve their denominational system.

We all need to model spiritual integrity and respect for the way God has wired us to receive the rewards of our Christian service in this world. God has not placed us in a rat race where what we need is spaced more and more infrequently the longer we serve God. God continues to lead us beside the still waters when we need our souls restored and our emotional energy reclaimed (Psalm 23:2-3). God desires for us to find weekly refreshment in worship, daily peace in devotion, and the needed rest for restoring both our souls and our relationships.

Leadership Lesson Number One

Good Leaders Are Honest about Their Own Limitations and Seek the Long Term Health and Spiritual Vitality of Their Coworkers

Self-care and compassion for others goes hand-in-hand. If I am giving 110 percent, then I may resent my coworkers who lack my unhealthy level of commitment. Those who are most compassionate are also those who are healthy in their own self-care and are willing to admit their own limitations.

— Evaluation Exercise —

AM I BURNED-OUT?

The following exercise is based upon the four types of Christian workers presented presented in this introduction, beginning on page 20. For each of the four categories, check as many lines as appropriately describe your life experiences this past week.

1) Healthy:

____ I maintain healthy spirituality through daily devotions and worship time.

____ I set aside a day this week in which I did not work or receive email or phone calls related to work.

____ I am willing to say no to requests that require me to work outside of my own spiritual gifts, temperament, or creative interests.

____ I found refreshment and an opportunity to praise God during worship this week.

____ I feel happy and satisfied with most days' accomplishments.

2) Accepting the Rat Race:

____ I look for scattered moments to pray or think about God, but I do not find the time for a regular devotional period each day.

____ I did not have a full day apart from work this week. I felt that I had to respond to email or phone calls even though I physically was not at the church on my day off.

____ I have a hard time saying no to someone who needs my help.

____ I was too busy to find refreshment or an opportunity to praise God during worship this week.

____ I feel frustrated that I never get done the things I need to do each day.

3) Experiencing Burnout:

____ I am becoming aware that something has to change or I won't be able to continue as I am in my church work.

____ I find that I am snapping more often and getting angry with others or myself.

____ Lately, I have felt depressed or vaguely exhausted.

____ I know I need to take more time off, but this week was worse than normal.

____ I am looking for a way to please the people who say that I work too hard.

4) Terminally Burned-Out:

____ I am preparing to, or have already, left my ministry and/or the church.

____ If I won the lottery, I would quit ninety percent of what I am doing with the church.

____ I have given up on worship; it is something I just go through without any feelings.

____ The only thing that keeps me going is that I don't want to be too much of a disappointment to others.

____ I no longer care about my church.

5) On the Road to Renewal

____ I recently made a firm commitment to have daily devotions and personal worship time.

____ I now am committed about honoring my Sabbath and have set aside a day this week in which I did not work or receive email or phone calls related to work.

____ I am going to therapy and/or am doing appropriate actions to deal with any depression, anger, anxiety, or unexpressed guilt that is driving my life away from the inner harmony I desire.

____ I am preparing to go on a personal retreat, or have begun journaling, or have otherwise set aside time to discover my own spiritual gifts, temperament, or creative interests.

____ I found new refreshment worshiping God this week.

Note the number of check marks beside each of the five categories. Where are you on this continuum?

1) Healthy

2) Accepting the Rat Race

3) Experiencing Burnout

4) Terminally Burned-Out

5) On the Road to Renewal

If you find yourself in the process of burnout, which of Dr. Külber-Ross five stages most fits your current life experience?

____ denial

____ anger (sub-stages below)

____ anger that is unexpected

____ anger that is directed towards those that are at fault

____ bargaining

____ depression

____ acceptance/implementation

CHAPTER ONE

The Problem with Perfection

"I'm going out to fish," Simon Peter told them, and they [six other disciples] said, "We'll go with you." So they went out and got into the boat, but that night they caught nothing.

John 21:3

The final pages of John's gospel find Peter in a funny place, his old fishing boat. Not that you wouldn't expect this most famous of fishermen to be fishing, it's just that you don't expect to find him doing that now, here, in the weeks following the first Easter. Jesus has just conquered death. The good news, which up to this point Peter and the other fishermen have been laboring to grasp, has just been put on display and made simple to believe. The good news now just needs to be announced. The church is waiting to be born and Peter knows that his job is to provide the foundation (the rock of certainty) for the new organization to stand on. Yet, Peter is not doing that; Peter is fishing.

You have to suspect burnout when a person who is known for his loyalty, who is committed to the importance of his work, and who has been trained well, does other things instead of the task that he has been assigned. Peter is in his old fishing boat because he doesn't have the heart to be out there on the road of discipleship doing his job. Going to the lake and baiting a few hooks may be an escape for Peter, just as it is for many people today, but this looks to me like something more. This is what psychologists call regression. Peter is going backwards. The last time we saw Peter in his boat was when Jesus first called him to follow and to walk on the pathway of making disciples. The very nature of Peter's relationship with Jesus is tied to the day, which we will look at later, when Jesus invited him to leave behind the nets and be a leader in the very public ministry of bringing salvation to people. Peter is returning to the comforts of an old familiar life, just as a person who has been beat up in the world will retreat to the safety of home.

Of course we can sympathize. Since the Palm Sunday entrance into Jerusalem a few weeks back, Peter and the others have been under a lot of stress. What we call "Holy Week" has been for them a series of twelve-hour days doing ministry in the midst of the city's crowds. These were followed each night by untold hours of Jesus seeking to cram final lessons into their weary skulls. Then on Thursday evening, when they were all ready to say, "Thank God it's Friday!" Jesus pulls an all-nighter. You know what happened next. The tensions of living in a place that had just carried out a raid, mock trial, and execution of their boss dogged their steps. Peter and the other disciples experienced personal uncertainly and conflict as they remained in Jerusalem addressing the questions and rumors that circulated among the crowds. If you have ever been in a workplace where there was a merger, bankruptcy, or hostile takeover, you know the tension such uncertainty generates. Peter and his friends carried the good news of Jesus' resurrection in the same hearts that also held the fears of being arrested, tried, and crucified. As I mentioned in my introduction, being of two minds is inherently exhausting.

As we go about the work of the church, we carry in our hearts the good news of the kingdom of God as well as the bad news of the church's financial problems, petty conflicts, miscommunications, and inability to recruit the right people for programs. Peter carried an additional burden. He had denied Jesus three times. Up until then, he had prided himself on being the top disciple. He was aiming for perfection and hoped to achieve it in this lifetime. In addition to his problem in admitting for whom he worked, Peter fell asleep on the job and used his sword to endanger the well-being of a minor. He now felt like he didn't deserve this job that he wasn't being paid to do. He was kind of glad that the boss wasn't around as much as before.

The good news of the church triumphant is often at odds with the bad news of the current state of affairs in the particular church we serve. We, like Peter, become tired of this oscillation between hope and despair. Many people experience the same loss of confidence in their own abilities, just as Peter did. We know in one part of our mind that we are doing the job that no one else would possibly want to do, and yet we can't shake the feeling that we aren't qualified or fit to do it. We may also come to realize that we aren't being as creative and putting out the high quality performance that we once did. On the other hand, aging pastors may resent how quickly the young are being promoted to the plum churches and denominational offices. Church staff find themselves wondering if the grass is greener in another parish, and then feel guilty for having such disloyal thoughts. Meanwhile, all of those who work for the church will find themselves feeling at some point ambivalent about their paycheck. We might say to ourselves, "I know that I am worth more, but I am doing this work for God and I feel bad about taking money from the church at all." The inconsistent and often backhanded way many congregations have of expressing appreciation for their leadership exacerbates these feelings.

Where do all of these feelings of ambivalence come from? Part of my own personal recovery started with a recognition that my own need to be perfect and my unwillingness to set reasonable boundaries around my employment harkened back to my childhood. I followed in the footsteps of my father who had a similar work addiction. I can also note places where my own lack of emotional security, coupled with theological misunderstanding, enhanced my unhealthy need to be needed (codependence) and my inordinate desire to please others. From the first time he invited Jesus into his boat, there already were in Peter's heart the seeds of his later perfectionism, work addiction, codependence, and unwillingness to set healthy emotional boundaries. As we shall see, from day one Jesus is teaching Peter another way of thinking. I believe that his words can guide us towards a more grace-filled way of working in his church.

But before we leave the twenty-first chapter of John, we should note how the following truths relate to our own experience of burnout and our hopes for finding healing:

- The fact that half of Jesus' disciples went out and got into that boat with Peter reminds us that the burnout of signifi-cant leaders has a tendency to diminish the commitment of others around them.

- Jesus did not respond to this fishermen's mutiny by yelling at them or firing the lot. Instead, he made them breakfast (John 21:12). He accepted their burnout and ministered to their needs.

- Jesus directly ministered to Peter's guilt over denying him three times by giving Peter the opportunity to confess his love three times. Guilt and the feeling that we are failing to meet expectations are significant contributors to burnout.

- Jesus reminded Peter that he was no longer a fisherman, but a shepherd of people. At some point we have to think about our past, come to accept it, and move on to the new future God has for us.

Peter's Calling

Matthew and Luke wait until the end of their fourth chapters to tell us how Peter became a follower of Jesus. I think they depart from Mark here because they want their readers to be aware that the real actor on the stage is God. Peter, indeed, had very little to do with Jesus' initial success. Multitudes came to hear Jesus and witness his miracles, includ-ing the healing of Peter's own mother-in-law (Luke 4:38-39). One has to wonder if Peter was too busy with his fishing business to pursue spir-itual things before Jesus came along. So Jesus takes his mission to the lakeshore, steps into Peter's boat, and sits down on the man's bait bucket. Peter, his hands smelling of fish-slime, hears this respected rabbi speak to the people about how the kingdom of God was in their midst. How did Peter respond to this tackle box teacher?

> When Simon Peter saw this, he fell at Jesus' knees and said, "Go away from me, Lord; I am a sinful man!" (Luke 5:8)

It is obvious that Peter is not having difficulty recognizing Jesus as Lord, nor is Peter denying his own personal need for salvation. I think Peter tells Jesus to get lost because he is full of doubt and shame. Like many people today, he thinks that he is not yet a good enough person to receive God. He wants to go home and put a suit on. He wants to pay back the debt he owes to the butcher and resolve the argument he had with his wife that morning. He wants to take back the swear words he said when the nets got tangled. He wants to quit smoking and become more faithful in his synagogue attendance. His mind is full of unmet expectations. He needs more time. He's not perfect yet.

I don't think that there was some dark secret sin that made Peter fearful. Some of us have heard old-time evangelists ask the question, "If you were to leave this place tonight and go out on the highway and be struck by a truck, would you be ready to meet the Lord?" Behind that question is the assumption that some sin, like murder, adultery, or drug addiction, is what separates us from spiritual contentment and finding a friend in Jesus. But for most of us, and I believe for Peter, it is the simple lack of our own perfection. It is the unresolved argument, the unpaid account, the in-box full of uncompleted tasks that cause us to tell Jesus to get out of our boat. It would be nice if those feelings of shame and of not being perfect enough yet would disappear forever from our lives the moment we became Christians. In a perfect world, we would just sing "Amazing Grace" and believe it forever. Every Christian would experience for the rest of their days the unquestioning acceptance proclaimed in "Blessed Assurance." But this is not the world we live out our faith in. Note that Jesus doesn't lead Peter in a prayer of confession. Instead, Jesus invites Peter to simply follow him. We often miss the simplicity of this invitation. Jesus will deal with the ongoing sinfulness of Peter's life day-by-day. But at this moment, Jesus offers to Peter unconditional acceptance. The very fact that Jesus wants to enter into his life the way that it currently is spooks Peter. Jesus hears Peter's difficulty and says, "Don't be afraid." I suspect it took the next three years of teaching and relating with Jesus for Peter to unpack and fully receive those words and to let them heal his soul.

What about us? Imagine that thing which most symbolizes your current life status. For Peter, it was a bait bucket. Imagine Jesus, sitting down on the front seat of your life-symbol saying, "Don't be afraid." I believe we are called to live by grace and not by the demands of perfectionism. But our inner quest for perfection generates a strange sense of fear and it leads us to engage in crazy behavior and to set ourselves up to burnout.

As we will see later on, perfectionism may cause procrastination because we keep fiddling with a task and not completing it for fear that it won't be done perfectly. Perfectionism may cause us to miss out on things we enjoy doing like eating a favorite food, playing a round of golf, or making love with our spouse, because it is not the perfect time, weather, or mood. Perfectionism reduces the joy of our rewards and increases the self-imposed demands of our labor. Further, we often become disengaged and distant from others at those very moments when we need most to speak our minds. We fail to communicate and advance our relationships because we fear we do not have the perfect words to speak about our feelings or the right poetry to display our inner passions. Perfectionism further hamstrings our witness as Christians because we waste opportunities as we wait for a perfect moment.

Plato Vs. Jesus

I like to blame my own struggle with perfectionism on the Greek philosopher, Plato. It's a whole lot more convenient to blame this kind of thing on someone who has been dead for twenty-four-hundred years, rather than on Mom, Dad, or my third grade teacher who wanted me to spell perfectly. Note that I say this tongue in cheek. Plato is not to blame, but our whole Western culture followed the early church's lead in building our value system around his idea about there being "perfect forms." We live today with a "shame based" understanding of the human condition. Instead of seeing ourselves as good people who have fallen into sin and dependent upon the grace of a savior, we see ourselves as bad people who need to work towards the goodness of perfection.

Plato, if I may paraphrase him, said that for every thing there is a perfect idea of that thing, an unblemished form, and in our minds eye we know this perfect form. We take this perfect ideal or form and we use it to recognize the objects around us. We know that a dog is a dog because he somehow conforms to this form of dog-ness that we have in our unconscious mind. We also use this idealized form to judge not only the objects we encounter, but also other people and even ourselves. In our mind's eye there is a perfect image of what a wife is, what a son should be like, what it is to be a good neighbor, etc. We hold others and ourselves up to this concept of the perfect pastor, the perfect youth worker, the perfect church.

It is as if we all have this unseen twin who is the real child of our heavenly Father. He or she is perfect, and it is this good twin whom we know is really the recipient of God's love, not the messy person who we know ourselves to be. We read self-help books and take on unreasonable commitments because we want to be this perfect twin. Like anything that is ideal, becoming our perfect selves is an unattainable goal. Perfectionism is the mistaken notion that there is a life we ought to be living and the only reason we are not living it is because we are lazy or stupid or lack the will to be good. We sometimes use humor to deal with our conscious manifestations of perfectionism. We might cut ourselves some slack, saying "I'm only human," or "It's hard to fly like an eagle when you live among turkeys." But then our subconscious mind overrules our sense of humor and makes comparisons between our behavior and that of our ideal twin. Shame enters our self-perceptions and robs us of all the rewards of life and the joy we could be finding in our labor. We know that what is supposed to be preached from our pulpits is a gospel of grace and liberations from guilt, but sometimes what we hear in church reinforces the shame and commitment to perfectionism.

Perfectionist ideals are a trap. They lead us away from asking the real questions of discipleship. Jesus did not call Peter to be perfect; he called him to faithfully follow and to learn how to fish with compassion for the hearts of other sinners in need of a savior, just as he was. We are not called to be our good twin. We are not called to be people who have somehow made it to perfection. We are called to be disciples, which implies being learners; we are called on a journey. We are willing to admit to our own imperfection because it enables us to direct people over to our master. We are, as D.T. Niles put it, " . . . beggars showing other beggars where to find bread." Knowing that we are loved just as we are, we call others to also become disciples. We depend each day on Jesus teaching us how to love the people we meet, as he would love them. This humble mindset is very much in contrast with the perfection seeking, shame-filled mind that lives in jealousy of the imaginary good twin.

By putting into our minds a philosophy that sounds Christian but isn't, Platonic perfectionism sets up a situation of two minds, which is inherently exhausting. We have the grace-filled mind, the heart that trusts in the saving merit of Jesus' atonement and sanctifying power of the Holy to guide us into humble paths of service and compassion. Then we have the perfectionist, self-righting mind, which castigates us with images of how much better our imaginary twin is doing. The mind that has yielded to grace does not fear and is rewarded by the everyday miracles that occur as we work together in the church. The perfectionist mind, however, expects things to constantly improve and is only rewarded when we surprise ourselves by exceeding expectations. Since these rewards come along very rarely, perfectionism will always lead to burnout. It is only a matter of time.

The Perfect Church

The church is also not called to be perfect, rather a loving refuge for sinners seeking the grace of God. Many congregations adopt perfectionist standards for measuring their achievements. Their leaders say things like:

- We will be a good church if we have consistent worship services where nothing goes wrong. We need this church to be a

place where the choir sings on key, the kids don't misbehave, and the pastor gets us out on time.

- We will be a good church if every Sunday school class is full and has perfect teachers who arrive prepared and on time.

- We will be a good church if we pay our denominational askings without complaint, fund a few missionaries, and have money left over at the end of the year to put into savings.

- We will be a good church if no one is unhappy and people get along without conflict.

The problem with these idealized understandings about what the church should be is that they distract us from discerning the leading of God's Spirit. We are so busy striving to become the perfect church that we fail to ask, "What does God want our congregation to be like?" or "What does God want us to be doing in mission to reach the people of our neighborhood?" Because we seek an idealized form of church life, we devalue the unique personality of our own congregation and rarely notice how indispensable our church may be in doing some particular outreach to our community. It is easy to see how congregations can become conflicted and burned-out when some people are striving to bring about perfection in worship, while others are striving to be perfect in stewardship, and another group is idealizing a fellowship without conflict, while a fourth group is only concerned about Christian education. Meanwhile, Jesus calls the church to spread the good news of God's kingdom and make disciples. It is inherently exhausting for a body to be of two minds, let alone of five minds. Jesus says:

> Come to me, all you who are weary and burdened, and I will give you rest. Take my yoke upon you and learn from me, for I am gentle and humble in heart, and you will find rest for your souls. For my yoke is easy and my burden is light (Matthew 11:28-30).

This beautiful promise leads me to think that Jesus did not intend his church to be exhausted, overcommitted, burdened, or perfect. If the church and her leaders become sensitive to the yoke they are supposed to engage or the task that Jesus has for this particular congregation, they won't become overtaxed. There will be resting times for the workers when they need it and the rewards of that labor will be sufficient to keep the leadership joyful. I believe Jesus made this promise of the easy yoke both for our corporate lives as congregations and for our individual lives as disciples.

The Early Church

The early church, as it moved into the Greek speaking and thinking world, baptized Plato and used his forms as a way of explaining sin, salvation, and the division of heaven and earth. In doing this, the church rejected the more natural definition of "perfection" offered by Aristotle. Aristotle said that within each thing, there is a goal, an end for which that thing was meant to be. Perfection is a matter of living into that goal. As humans we are not meant to be angels or to conform to any other imagined heavenly form. We are meant, instead, to gain maturity, to grow into the person God intended us to be, and to learn how to love one another. God calls us to live creatively and playfully in the midst of this world with all of its uncertainty, controversy, and imperfection. With all that is ambiguous about us, it is impossible for us to be right. Instead, we must strive to head in the right direction and rejoice in those moments when we see love and God's grace leading our way.

I am not saying that Plato was all wrong and that Aristotle was the perfect philosopher. However, much of what is wrong with the church today can be traced back to the platonic way of seeing things. The question I wish to raise is how does your congregational leadership see the world?

- Do you see it as a place where we are stuck? Are our perfection-desiring souls trapped here until Jesus returns for us or until we die and then, as the old hymn puts it, "I'll fly away." If so, you lean toward Plato and the dangers of perfectionism robbing you of the rewards God has placed in the midst of this world.

- If, leaning towards Aristotle, you see the world as a place that was made good in its diversity, with each individual and creature having their own way of becoming mature, then you will expect ambiguity, uncertainty, controversy, conflict, and imperfection as natural consequences of the complexity of life. Heaven will be the goal of our journey and getting there will be half the fun, rather than a place we Christians are hoping to escape to.

- Plato's psychology tended to see the soul and the body as separate entities, which could even be in conflict with each other. Today in the church we sometimes mistakenly deny the body's needs for rest and exercise because we think we can perfect the soul separate from the body.

- Aristotle influences modern medicine more as it sees the mind and the soul (Greek word "psyche") integrated with the body. Physical health, mental health, and spiritual soulfulness are once again being joined, just as they are in the ancient Hebrew concept of Shalom.

- When platonic thought dominates the church, we retreat from the world and seek a separate spirituality. Congregations with a platonic mindset are afraid to take on new members who don't perfectly agree with the church's theology. They often separate themselves from other denominations that don't accept their particular path to perfection.

- On the other hand, churches that are dominated by aristotelian thought feel driven into the marketplace of ideas. They are not only seeker friendly, but they see themselves as still seeking. For Aristotle, the perfect person is the one who has discovered the goal of life and what it means to live a virtuous life, and then tries to guide the political structures of the community so that others may enjoy that life. It is based upon the concept of becoming fully human, rather than on becoming fully perfect.

The last image we have of Plato is of him preparing to drink hemlock poison in Athens rather than escaping to the islands for the sabbatical his students had prepared for him. In holding onto perfection and his philosophical ideals, he makes a dramatic exit and achieves martyrdom. This is certainly the thing to do if you want to be remembered centuries later, and to this day the action strikes Philosophy 101 students and theologians as being almost Christ-like. It has taken me a long time to realize that we are called to be Christ-like in our love, not in our stubbornness for perfectionist ideals or our desire to be famous martyrs. As we shall see throughout this book, the unconscious desire to be a martyr fuels many of the self-defeating and perfectionist behaviors that lead us inevitably to burnout.

Platonic perfectionism even redefines the way we pray. Jesus taught and modeled a simple and practical approach to prayer. He said to begin with one of the first words a child learns to speak, *abba*, or "father." Short sentences then proceed to tie together our earthly needs and God's generous promises. But the spirit of perfection shifts our attention away from God's willingness to accept and hear us and instead focuses on having the perfect words, the proper theology, and the most solemn voice for our prayers. The platonic prayer speaks about disembodied ideals rather than the nitty-gritty details of our current lives and social context. It speaks about the church in general, rather than our own congregation and its struggles. Further, whenever the demands of perfectionism creep into my own devotional life, I find myself inserting an extra line into the Lord's Prayer: "Give us this day the time we need to do the things we've got to do." Notice that the real Lord's Prayer contains petitions for our daily bread and for strength when tempted, but says nothing at all about needing more time. Nor does Jesus teach us to ask God to make us perfect.

"Yes, But . . . "

Doesn't Jesus somewhere call us to be perfect? Each pastor who is ordained in The United Methodist Church is asked a series of questions that include: "Are you going on to perfection? Do you expect to be made perfect in love in this life? Are you earnestly striving after perfection in love?" (par 330.d, 2004 *The Book of Discipline*). These questions harken back to John Wesley's concern that Christians who cease to strive to become better and more holy people soon cease to be faithful altogether. The type of perfection John Wesley and the church were looking for is "perfection in love." Wesley's thought was much more in debt to Aristotle than Plato, in that he saw being holy as something that was active and changing. We become perfect as people not when we, like angels, stop doing anything wrong, but when we become fully human in our love and in our compassion for others.

None of us will ever be perfect in knowledge or right behavior, but we have a hope and a desire to love people the way Christ loves them. When we treat someone exactly as Jesus would have treated him or her, in that moment, we are perfect.

There are two places where Jesus speaks about perfection and it is important to see each in its context. The first relates to the concept of striving to be more loving towards other people:

> But I tell you: Love your enemies and pray for those
> who persecute you, that you may be sons of your Father
> in heaven . . . Be perfect, therefore, as your heavenly
> Father is perfect (Matthew 5:44-45a, 48).

In the second text, Jesus is being very Aristotelian in challenging a young individual to towards the goal of what God had planned for him as a human being.

> Jesus answered, "If you want to be perfect, go, sell your
> possessions and give to the poor, and you will have
> treasure in heaven. Then come, follow me" (Matthew
> 19:21).

We all want to be perfect. Jesus doesn't tell us to find perfection by conforming ourselves into some perfect ideal human being, by following all the advice found in self-help books, or by spending twenty-four hours a day frantically trying to be all things to all people. One finds perfection by acting with sincere love and charity towards those around us and by following our particular vocation or calling for life. For this young man, following Jesus and being a disciple would not have made him perfect according to any platonic ideal. Instead it would have put him in a place where God would have shows God's perfect grace. God does perfect things with frail, sinful, and imperfect mortals like you and me. We remain imperfect, but God allows us to experience moments when we have the joy of loving others as Christ would love them, and moments when we are in the right place and doing the right thing because we have simply lived our vocation as God took our humble efforts and blessed them.

It is for us just as God says it to Paul, "My grace is sufficient for you, for my power is made perfect in weakness" (Second Corinthians 12:9).

The Perfect Game

When our children were small we gave them a game called Perfection. It was a plastic box with odd shaped holes in which you had to place matching odd shaped blocks. To be perfect you had to place all the blocks in their matching holes within a given time. Hidden within the plastic box there was a timer, constantly ticking. When you failed to get all the pieces in their places before the timer dinged, the box erupted, scattering the blocks. Perfection is one of those "educational games" that well-meaning parents give their children for the parents' amusement. My wife and I received a great deal of amusement from watching our children try harder and harder to complete a task that was so much like life. The game models the trap of perfection. From the moment one begins to play, there is a clear understanding of what perfection is. The goal is to have all the pieces safely placed in their sockets. But as the game progresses, an overwhelming barrage of details intrudes. We become aware of the ticking of the clock. Time and life's interruptions become our enemies.

Perfection is a hard game to play. In both our individual lives and our corporate life as a congregation, three behaviors become habitual, pervasive, and reveal the pursuit of perfection:

- Rigidity and loss of humor—the valuing of perfection means a denial of the irony and ambiguity that makes life fun.

- Procrastination—wanting to do our tasks perfectly means they never get done on time.

- Unwillingness to try new things—the fear of failing to be perfect and the stress of seeking a clean desk causes one to see innovation as a luxury.

When Jesus says, "Don't be afraid," he is not only calling us to receive the fact that we are forgiven, he is also calling us to question the self-expectations we may have inherited from our childhood. The word *grace* (literally meaning "gift") deals with more than just the gift of getting faults forgiven. It also deals with being given a new standard by which to live. Jesus calls us to be his human disciples, emphasizing love, forgiveness, and learning from our mistakes over perfection. Grace invites us to realize that the whole game of perfectionism is ill conceived.

The church today often teaches the right theology (that is the right understanding of God's grace), but then fails to back this teaching up with tools for recovery. Not only do we need to know the meaning of grace, we also need to develop habits that enable us to cut ourselves some slack. For many people, being a perfectionist is a life-long habit, a character flaw best handled with therapy. My sense is that most churches today have fallen into a dualism where they recognize and teach in liturgy and sermons the gracious gospel of Christ, but in membership expectations, policies, and day-to-day practices, there is a deeper sub-message of perfectionism. This may be why some people who enter therapy for codependence or into a twelve-step program for addiction find they feel uncomfortable in their home congregation and quietly drop out of church for a while.

Rigidity

One of the things I have noticed both as a pastor and as a church consultant is that some congregations are more "fun" than others. This may seem an unfair generalization, but some churches have a certain stiff and humorless rigidity to their fellowship or the way they conduct business. Have you ever been a guest at a home when one of the children has made some mistake, such as spilling milk? If the family is "normal," this incident will be handled with a bit of humor and the minimum of fuss. But if there is something amiss in the family, the minor incident may either become a major one, or it might be rigidly ignored. The normal home flexes and bends with each individual, making varying demands for the attention of the whole. In the same sense, the normal church provides flexibility and a sense of humor to smooth edges when something unexpected happens. They have come to accept that not every program or worship hour will go perfectly.

Rigidity often occurs in churches that have been traumatized by clergy misconduct or have a history of conflict. Adopting a rigid way of doing things becomes a defensive mechanism against further trauma. I know of one church that spent endless hours developing policies concerning the proper use of the church kitchen and what outside groups must pay in rental. Such busyness about minor issues kept them from looking at the more serious issues of their changing neighborhood and the trauma of losing a beloved pastor. Perfectionism is sometimes a symptom of something deeper, but what is important to consider in the context of burnout is how such behavior robs church leaders of the joy they should be experiencing in their work. When a church is not fun, it is not fun.

Perfectionism and Procrastination

We may blame our poor organization skills, but that annoying habit of putting things off until the last moment is usually related to perfectionism. There is a scene in the movie *Six Degrees of Separation* (screenplay by John Guare, Metro-Goldwyn Mayer, 1993) in which a grade school art teacher is asked why the works of her students are so much better than the works of others in the same grade. She responds, "It's because I know when to take their papers away from them." The implication is that the children spoil their own art by trying too hard to make it perfect. When something is done we need to stop. But when is anything ever really done?

There is always a certain amount of arrogance when we procrastinate in order to make something perfect. We lose perspective on how what we are doing relates to the whole. There are tasks in life that require a week's worth of thought and effort. There are tasks that require a day and others which require an hour. If in our arrogance we spend a week on activities that deserve a day, or a day on activities that deserve an hour, then we are being irrational.

PERFECTIONISM AND THE UNWILLINGNESS TO TRY

The kissing cousin to procrastination is the lack of initiative to attempt new things. Why is it that burned-out people become unwilling to try new things and display a loss of creativity? Although we value innovation and risk-taking in others, we may consider it a luxury in our own lives. When stress causes us to shut down and behave defensively, we consider curiosity and inventiveness unnecessary risks. We fall back to rigid, predictable behavior and familiar ways of doing things. This not only surfaces in our actions as congregational leaders, but also can become a broad cultural trait of a church that has fallen into a perfection driven mode of operation.

Everyone expects a certain learning curve when attempting new things. Perfectionists, however, fear even their initial showing might be embarrassing. They don't want to look bad as they experiment with a new skill. In a similar fashion, being innovative and creative as a church leader involves risks because unexpected outcomes may mar the perfection one is trying to achieve. The motto of perfectionists everywhere is, "If I can't do it well (translate "perfectly"), I won't do it at all."

In order to avoid burnout we must learn that in our church work we are not like figure skaters being judged on the basis of how close we come to giving a perfect performance. Instead, like most things in life, we are judged and compensated on the basis of what the community needs. A farmer who raises bushels of near perfect zucchini should not take it personally if people are not willing to buy something that his or her own gardens are producing too much of. Yet, it is the nature of perfectionists to take everything personally.

There are some things in life that are purely meant to be a gift. A game of golf, unless you are Tiger Woods, is meant to be a time of recreation and relaxation. It becomes work if you judge every stroke by how the ball should have been hit if you were perfect. Some of us make ourselves sick by working at our play. By constantly working for perfection, we exhaust the gift latent in a playful act. The calmness that is inherent in the things we do for recreation can be stolen by our perfectionism.

Perhaps it is in the area of recreation that the difference between grace and guilt-driven perfectionism becomes most obvious. Grace enables golfers to smell the new mown grass, feel the rhythm of their muscles contributing each in turn to form an arc, address the ball, and hear this sound of its departure. By grace, golfers are present to companions, engaging in the flow of conversation. They give and take affirmation and acceptance from this fellowship. One can still have the joy of competition and desire to see one grow in understanding the game. But the grace of the game lies somewhere deeper than the score. Games that are worthy of lifelong pursuit are not mastered. Mastery is a perfectionist (and sexist) term. Instead, one senses the appropriateness of the day in refreshing one's soul, and leaves the green with a new appreciation of the nuance of the game.

Now in the above paragraph, substitute your position in the church for the words relating to golf and try to rewrite the lines to reflect how grace can be a part of your daily activity. If you are a pastor, then the paragraph above may read:

Perhaps it is in the area of pastoral service that the difference between grace and guilt-driven perfectionism is most obvious. Grace enables the pastor to see the beauty of the sanctuary and enjoy the rhythm of his or her voice leading the psalms and contributing to the worship experience. By grace, the pastor is present to the other church leaders, engaging in the flow of conversation. He or she gives and takes affirmation and acceptance from this fellowship.

BLESSINGS IN THE MOMENT

The key issue of perfectionism is the way one doesn't accept the blessing of what is. Hope for life beyond burnout involves refocusing on the here and now. Perfectionists foolishly strive an idealized life, even if that image has no basis in this earthly existence. We want the perfect family, the perfect wardrobe, the perfect car, the perfect church, the perfect pastor. Whether we want to admit it or not, perfectionism is almost always closely related to our need to control others, or at least control the image we project to the world (see the next chapter on codependency). We often ruin relationships and fail to treat others lovingly because we are stuck on rigid, perfection-driven expectations. We all need a certain amount of rules and structure in order to keep our lives from chaos. But if we loose our spontaneity, then we are not open to the grace of what happens moment-by-moment.

This may be what Jesus was saying when he preached "the kingdom of God is among you" (Luke 17:21 NRSV). God's kingdom is not found in some platonic world of the forms where the ideal family or church exists. It is instead found in the grace of this moment; in this very moment God is speaking acceptance of you. The kingdom of God is not something found in the future when finally we get our act together. The kingdom of God is now in the midst of the church, with all of its imperfections. To follow Jesus means having to give up on trying to become perfect by one's own means. If I choose to follow Jesus, then I must abandon my quest for my own imaginary forms of perfectionism. We must choose the gift of grace over the burden of good intentions.

Grace has little to do with how we stand in relationship to some external standard of perfection. It has everything to do with the capacity we have right now, this moment, to respond to God's call on our lives. We are in every moment like Peter in the boat with Jesus. We can either reject the current set of opportunities that life gives us because we are afraid that we are a sinner, or we can accept this moment as the moment of God's call. Grace is the one thing that can bring peace to the soul and replace the hopeless game of perfectionism.

Who Is to Blame?

We often speak about how difficult it must have been for Peter and the others to leave behind their nets and simply follow Jesus. We assume they struggled hard with the decision to leave behind their families and the regular income that fishing provided. But who knows how they really felt? That morning, when Jesus sat down on Peter's bait pail, Peter might have been ready for a change. Picture him with his back aching from hauling up empty nets all night and the lack of sleep addling his brain. His wife might have been nagging him to get a job with better hours and more money. Peter might have been wondering just how he was going to pay the big increase in his leaky boat's tax assessment when he heard Jesus say, "Come follow me." He might have gladly jumped at the chance to work the daylight shift. If this is true, then in three short years we see Peter going from being a burned-out fisherman to being a burned-out disciple.

This returns us to the question of where to place the blame for burnout. Burnout is often seen as the consequence of a flaw or weakness in the character of the individual. Was it possible that Peter was weaker than the others and lacked the stamina that we later see demonstrated in Paul? In the church, we often praise those who make themselves into martyrs. We have a long-running love affair with expectations of perfection in people. When someone backs off from taking on an additional job in the church, we often question his or her commitment or Christian maturity. Many of us bear the scars of being told it was our fault for becoming burned-out. A wiser approach is to see that some of our individual traits, such as the propensity towards perfectionism, the proneness to work addiction, and a weakness for codependent relationships, make us vulnerable to burnout. It doesn't do anyone any good to blame themselves for reaching that stage in ministry where he or she feels like dropping out.

The opposite solution is to blame the job or the church. In the secular world, we see articles proclaiming the high rate of burnout among dentists, lawyers, postal workers, etc. Each occupation has its own form of stress and its own traditions for dealing with or ignoring the pain of those who find their physical or emotional health seriously jeopardized by their working environment. In the church, just as in other workplaces, we can become aware that what we are being asked to do for the sake of the institution is in conflict with our basic human values or with what is healthy for us. Back in the 1970s, IBM managers complained that the corporate name really meant "I've Been Moved" because commitment to the company meant being willing to be uprooted every two to three years. For people with an internal value of home stability and extended family relationships, this meant work conflicted with who they were. Clergy often reach the place were they put the entire blame for their burnout on the institution and come to think their feelings are unique to their profession. I have been careful in this book to say that the factors that contribute to burnout affect everyone in church leadership. Congregations can develop an unhealthy culture and drive both their paid staff and volunteers crazy. Further, denominations can enact policies and promote hierarchical ways of thinking that both increases the drop-out rate of their pastors and makes the institution more vulnerable to the high costs of clergy misconduct, addiction, and health related disabilities.

A third way of seeing burnout is to place the blame on a mismatch between the worker and the job. This is what Maslach and Leiter mean when they define burnout as a "dislocation between what people are and what they have to do" [*The Truth About Burnout: How Organizations Cause Personal Stress and What to Do About It* by Christina Maslach and Michael P. Leiter (Jossey-Bass, 1997),17]. The problem with seeing this as the entire solution to the question of burnout is that people who are perfectly suited to their task still often get burned-out. When we first find that a job clicks with us, our impulse is to throw ourselves into the work. We set perfectionist-driven standards for our productivity, we allow ourselves to become workaholics, and we overcommit and agree to codependent relationships. All the things that make for burnout can be experienced in even the most perfect job.

I am not comfortable with fixing the blame for burnout on the individual, the church, or on even an interaction between the two. Burnout is, as stated before, a state of awareness where what we are doing is no longer working for us and we can no longer accommodate the exhaustion of being of two minds. We need to be re-tooled and re-defined, and perhaps as Peter was at the end of John's gospel, re-called to our true vocation. We each bring into adulthood certain vulnerabilities—some to perfectionism, others to work addiction, codependence, and overload. There comes a point when the course of our lives needs radical readjustment. The awareness that accompanies burnout, then, works within God's greater plan for our good. The church is not a perfect institution and each congregation has its way of aggravating, and sometimes manipulating for its own ends, the inherent weaknesses of workers. There are times when the church is more interested in being perfect than in being a place of healing and spiritual self-discovery. With all these things in mind, we need to work together to fix the problem rather than fix the blame.

How Not To Be Perfect

More than the other causes of burnout that we will deal within subsequent chapters, overcoming the need to be perfect requires a radical change in thinking. Where we once associated being good with being perfect, we need now to associate goodness with the flexibility to be both human and grace dependent in our work. In both our individual lives and our communal life, the roots of perfectionism run deep. For many of us, disarming our internal drive to be perfect will require therapy as well as a rediscovery of the forgiving nature of our Lord. Much more could and should be said on this subject, but for now we must simply imagine Jesus sitting upon our bait box and calling us to an imperfect life of discipleship, with the admonition to be not afraid.

Leadership Lesson Number Two

Good Leaders don't seek to be right; they seek to be Christ-like.

Good leaders are not people who are always right or who are always making the right decisions. Good leaders lead others towards living up to their full potential. They focus on the goal of Christ-like love, rather than the many goals of everyone's expectations.

— Evaluation Exercise —

HOW MUCH OF A PERFECTIONIST AM I?

1) Is the amount of time or attention you devote to doing things "just right" an underlying theme in the conflicts you have with your spouse, friends, or co-workers?

   Never   Sometimes   Frequently

2) Are there nights that you have difficulty sleeping because you can't stop thinking about something you have not done well or completed perfectly?

   Never   Sometimes   Frequently

3) Do you devote more attention to certain tasks than your job allows and so end up spending more time at work than others expect you to?

   Never   Sometimes   Frequently

4) Are you often fearful that a job you have done will reflect badly on you?

   Never   Sometimes   Frequently

Answering positively to any of the above questions is a serious indicator that perfectionism is in control of your life. Think about the questions you have checked as indicators of places you have sacrificed your own happiness for a philosophy that does not fit with your humanity.

— Evaluation Exercise —

HOW DEEPLY DOES YOUR CHURCH BUY INTO PERFECTION?

1) In the last several months, has the need to do things "right" or with "quality" caused hurt feelings or led to conflict between church leaders?

No   Some minor friction   Yes

2) Are there nights that you have difficulty sleeping because you are concerned that your efforts will not meet the expectations of other key church leaders?

Never   Sometimes   Frequently

3) Is it just generally assumed that every church worker will put in more hours than they are compensated for and/or that the pastors will not take their full vacations or weekly days off?

No   Maybe   Yes

4) When workers and volunteers miss programs or committee meetings because of family concerns or illness, is their level of commitment to the church questioned by other leaders?

No   Sometimes   Frequently

— **Practical Exercise** —

For one week, pray the Lord's Prayer three times a day. Pray it slowly. Notice the emphasis upon this world and this day. Do not pray it as a means of getting heavenly brownie points. Do not pray it as a preface to your own request for more time and money to do what you want to do. Instead, pray it as a blessing upon your current life, with all its faults. This prayer is a gift, not given to the perfect, but to those who wish to live fully by God's grace in the here and now.

CHAPTER TWO

Sink First, Ask Questions Later

"You're so vain, I bet you think this song is about you."

"You're So Vain", Carly Simon, 1972

Jesus did many things to prevent his disciples from becoming overly dependent upon him. He went into the hills to pray while they stayed behind to deal with things themselves. He booked alternate travel arrangements, sending the disciples ahead on the more adventurous route and forcing them to think for themselves. He left them alone to sink or swim on their own. This predilection for forcing independence set the stage for that dark and stormy night when Peter decided to walk on water.

> . . . the boat was already a considerable distance from land, buffeted by the waves because the wind was against it. During the fourth watch of the night Jesus went out to them, walking on the lake . . . (Matthew 14:24-25).

Who has any doubt that Peter was captaining the boat just before Jesus stepped in? He was the natural leader, and he, like many of us, assumed that being a leader meant answering every question and fixing every problem. The disciples had come to lean on Peter and he, I am sure, had come to enjoy that. Like many church leaders today, I picture Peter taking full responsibility and refusing to share the load. If there is only one oar in the boat, Peter will have it. If there is only one bucket to bail with, Peter will have it in his other hand. If the boat sinks, Peter has already decided to go down with the ship. Churning in the back of his mind is the gallant hope that he can still be the savior of this cruise. For the last three hours Peter has been preaching to the crew that the wind, waves, and darkness, are only figments of their unbelieving minds, that the only thing they should fear is fear itself. He is about to be sunk by his own sermon when Jesus finally shows up. Instead of relaxing, Peter reaches for something else that he can do to show his commitment to the cause. He calls out, "Lord, if it's you . . . tell me to come to you on the water" (Matthew 14:28).

We usually look at this passage as an example of heroic faith, but in this chapter I want to flip it over and see the other side. Instead of thinking about Peter as a courageous saint, let us picture him as a church leader like you and me. How often have we felt compelled to do foolish things in order to prove our worthiness to be in charge? The frantic need to fix even un-fixable situations is common among clergy and active laity today. We throw ourselves into saving dwindling programs, often becoming the only people supporting the effort. We tweak our statistical reports and try to put forth the image of our church as a "growing church," even though it may in fact be declining. We take the storms and conflicts that swamp our little congregation personally, meeting late into the night to resolve issues. We worry about how things might look to outsiders. This constant need to save the church can be emotionally exhausting and can lead us to burnout.

Paul took a different tack when he was on a sinking ship (Acts 27:13-38). He watched calmly as the sailors threw overboard every non-essential item that was weighing the ship down. He led the people by restating the boat's priorities and a few common sense safety rules such as the importance of everyone staying on board. No water-walking for Paul. Then he gathered the people in prayer, gave them hope, and encouraged them to rest and eat. There are times in church life when we need to ride out the storm and be the calm voice of reason. Instead of being super heroes, we are called to be honest persons of faith.

The church, however, likes having impulsive fools like Peter. There is something in our social dynamic that always raises someone to be the class clown or the group's token martyr. The fact that someone is foolish enough to step out of the boat means the rest of us don't have to. The leadership role of "water-walker" is one that just begs to be filled. Clergy often feel pressure to model their faith more fervently than anyone else in the congregation. One pastor remarked, "My congregation pays me to be holy, so they don't have to."

Joe was the pastor of the main street church in a factory town. Concerned that some would think he was not working as hard as he should, he would arise at six in the morning, put on a suit, and stand on his porch, waving at the mill workers as they drove in for first shift. He was always the first to arrive on Sunday and the last to leave the building, joining his family long after the noon meal had grown cold. When church meetings ran late into the night, he would never be the one to complain about the time. Joe was obsessed that the blue-collar laity would think less of him and his profession because he did not work with his hands. In his spare time, toolbox in hand, he fixed whatever was broken around the church building. While many in the church saw this as an act, others would quietly stroke his vanity saying, "Pastor Joe, we can't get anything done around here without you!" Joe needed to be needed and worked long hours to cultivate this feeling of dependency among his followers.

A complex social system that develops a dependency relationship with one or two individuals is a house of cards. One day Pastor Joe will move on to another church, or as in the sad case of the person the above account is based upon, be forced to leave the ministry. Individuals who obsess over how they appear to others are building their self-esteem on shaky ground. The need to project a certain image, the need to fix things (or be a savior), and the need to be needed, form a three-fold concentration of neediness in the individuals and congregations who have forsaken the grace of God in an attempt to be appreciated by people for what they do. The cost of this trap is hard to estimate. It turns lesser things into priorities and keeps us from experiencing the simple joys of church life. The unfettered offering of our hearts in praise to God cannot happen when our minds are dwelling upon how we look. A loving fellowship cannot develop in a congregation when a few needy church leaders are constantly seeking to have the attention focus upon them. The priority of our family obligations and our own spiritual disciplines will be forsaken if we launch ourselves on the impossible quest of making ourselves indispensable at work.

Defining Codependence

There is a word for the group of psychological traits that I have been attributing to Peter and blaming for the "water-walking" behavior we often see in today's church. When an individual or organization is overly concerned with how things look, what they can fix, or who they can get to depend totally upon them, they are suffering from codependence. Codependence is a clinical term used to describe a person whose mental health seems to be trapped by unfulfilled childhood needs. In order to develop into an emotionally stable adult, children need the assurance that they are loved and accepted for being themselves, and not because they are needed to fix something. This unconditional love is indispensable for the formation of a personality that is not dependent upon what other people think.

The concept of codependence was first developed by researchers looking into the personality traits of adult children of alcoholics. In family systems, where one of the parents is addicted to a substance or has a behavioral addiction such as work-addiction, the other members of the family develop roles to compensate for the addict. These persons may enter into adulthood wanting to do in their church and other significant relationships something that they could not do in their family of origin—that is, fix the abuser. Codependents are perpetual caregivers and problem fixers. Further, because their family was too busy adjusting to the addicted parent to provide sufficient nurture and love, codependents feel a deep craving to have people like them. They are natural people pleasers. They can be extremely sensitive to the feelings of others, but totally oblivious to their own feelings or personal needs. There is a drive to their neediness.

As the concept of codependence has gained popularity over the last three decades, psychologists have begun to find these traits in people from a variety of backgrounds, not just adult children of alcoholics. In fact, authors such as Annie Wilson Schaef state that our culture itself is addictive and that each of us suffer to some degree from dysfunctional behaviors relating to our need to be needed [*Co-dependence: Misunderstood and Mistreated* by Annie Wilson Schaef (HarperCollins, 1986) and *The Addictive Organization: Why We Overwork, Cover Up, Pick Up the Pieces, Please the Boss, and Perpetuate Sick Organizations* by Annie Wilson Schaef and Diane Fassel (HarperCollins, 1988)]. Asking an American to describe the effect of this disorder is like asking a fish to describe water. What I want to point out is that some congregations are more prone than others to place extremely codependent people into leadership roles. Churches that have had some type of trauma, such as a pastoral misconduct or the unexpected loss of a beloved long-term pastor, may also display more obvious codependent characteristics.

When individuals fail to question codependent behavior or place limits on what we will do to please others, we set ourselves up for burnout. If causing people to be dependent upon us provides us with inappropriate psychological rewards, then we should be aware that these rewards will become more and more difficult to obtain the further we go in our church work. Like pastor Joe, we will find ourselves staying up late and rising early to get one more person to appreciate us, and tormenting ourselves when people don't sing our praises. Until we address these childhood issues, we will behave in increasingly self-destructive ways until we become burned-out.

Together, codependency and perfectionism (chapter one) form what I call the whipsaw of guilt. Imagine the old two-man saw working at a tree. The codependent part of our personality grips one side of the whipsaw saying, "I should be doing more." The perfectionist-driven side of our personality pulls back on the saw saying, "I won't do anything unless I can do it perfectly." Back and forth we oscillate between taking on more than we can do well and then feeling that we have to do what is on our plate to incredible standards. Like sawdust, anger accumulates from the unexpressed resentment inherent in this back and forth whipsaw.

BEING OURSELVES

Charles Dickens' book *David Copperfield* begins with this telling line: "Whether I shall turn out to be the hero of my own life or whether that station will be held by anyone else, these pages must show."

The greatest cost of codependence is that it keeps us from becoming the hero of our own lives. We seek so hard to build the esteem from others that we fail to notice what will satisfy our own appreciation of who we have become. Jesus constantly gave people back to themselves. When he spoke to the woman at the well (John 4:5-42) or freed the Gerasene demoniac from his affliction (Luke 8:26-39), he did not make these people to be needy sycophants. Instead, he freed them to be themselves.

When I was in full time ministry, I often complained that my parishioners were evenly divided into two unreasonable camps. First, there were those who believed I only worked one hour a week. Trying to convince them otherwise was like bailing the sea with a bucket. The second group held the opposite opinion and saw me as such a very busy man that I really didn't have time for them. They would hesitate to call me in times of crisis and leave me out of the loop in matters where I genuinely desired to be of service. This group broke my heart with their efforts not to infringe on my time. Worse yet, their opinion put them in conflict with the first group. I was constantly tempted to call upon them as my allies in my efforts to please the people who thought I only worked one hour a week.

Imagine my relief when I began to realize that these two groups of people were only a small minority in the church and in the world. Most people really don't have any idea or any concern about how many hours a week I work. They simply assume that if I am a dedicated and honest person I will work a normal week. Further, most people are too busy with their own lives to have even thought about my workweek. In turn, I should be more concerned about my own integrity and the legitimate business I have been given to do on this earth, than with what others think.

What I have come to realize now is that every effort at changing the ways others see us endangers our sanity. Sanity is that slippery sense of being at peace with ourselves, with the important people around us, and with God's plan for our life. If we have sanity, our efforts, our work, our rest, and our play all coordinate to foster loving relationships and to achieve life's goals. If we have crazyness, every labor pushes us further from understanding our true selves.

As Christians, we come to realize that our lives rarely seem to be sane without the quietude of prayer, for we need to tune our inner ears to hear God's higher calling in order to be at peace. Codependence has the effect of amplifying our concerns about the expectations of others while at the same time it plays havoc on our prayer lives Few people find sanity without radically divorcing themselves from the expectations of others. We have to force ourselves to come to not care what others think. We become free, like the child who cried that the emperor has no clothes, to state the truth we perceive rather than the one others want us to accept.

We are all self-conscious to some degree. We are afraid what others may think when they look at us. This concern for our personal image—our name, our reputation—is often unwarranted. Most of the time people are not aware of what we wore, what we said, or how we looked. When we become obsessed with how we appear to others we engage in exhausting behaviors and this, too, can contribute to burnout.

In a similar way, some local churches become overly concerned about how they appear. They may think they have a reputation as the first church of their city or as the plum church of their denomination. This vanity can distract the congregation's leaders and prevent them from discerning their real mission as a church. The congregation may find itself of two minds, one group being obsessed with how the church looks and what people are saying, and the other group earnestly desiring to discover how they can make disciples for Christ in their context. This friction will eventually tire people of both camps.

Getting Work Done

The church loves to hire seriously codependent people. These poor souls will readily work impossible hours just to please people and to feel needed. Not everyone who is codependent, however, is productive and few can maintain their high-speed dance of image control for long. In fact, like any psychological malady, codependence will eventually cause more harm than good.

Imagine the plight of a small city that has a long-term employee named Arlene. Arlene slumps around her city hall office like a troll amid the chaotic stacks of files. Your first thought is, "How can anyone find anything in this mess?" Arlene, however, can find any form or record instantly. She will not get you your form until you have visited her office three times and heard on each visit a rendition of how computers are ruining everything by eliminating the all-important human touch. The entire city depends on her, and if she ever called in sick, which she won't, workers would go unpaid and construction grind to a halt. Eventually Arlene will die or be forced to retire and it is doubtful anyone will remember how rarely she has asked for assistance, modern office equipment, vacation time, or a raise. But they will notice how she codependently made herself impossible to replace, and it will cost dearly to re-file, re-staff, and re-organize this office.

In the church, people like Arlene are legion. They chair trustee committees for decades, they keep membership or financial records in a way that no one else understands, and they are the pastors who no one wants to follow. They love the church, but they also love being in control and having people depend on them alone. The difficult thing is to help these people see they can be loved and respected without needing to be needed. The church is not going to be healthy if every decision needs to be run through them. It is hard to tell a codependent that what he or she thinks is exemplary Christian service, is actually an illness that needs treatment. When extreme codependents like Arlene become burned-out, and they always will, they sometimes dramatically implode, leaving the church with a mess. More often, they contribute a note of depression and resistance to change to every committee they sit upon.

Codependents harm the work of the church in three ways:

First, they insert discord and chaos into the organizational structure of the church. Codependents manipulate the decision making process of the church so everything has to pass through them. Church volunteers soon resent being in leadership roles and not being allowed to act until they get the approval of the codependent. The congregational system often becomes polarized with newcomers at odds with those people who are aligned with the codependent.

Second, they set a limit on what the church can accomplish. Because codependents are often burned-out, their energy level may be very low. They will resist allowing the church to do new things, even though there are other leaders to make it happen, because the codependent needs to be involved in everything.

Third, they make others feel guilty about their level of Christian service. No one can live up to the sacrifices being made by a full-blown, martyrdom-seeking codependent. Instead of focusing on the grace, love, and forgiveness of God, congregations dominated by codependents focus on perfection, excessive work, and on how things look.

Leadership Lesson Three

Good Leaders Develop Self-Sufficient Followers

The catch-and-release style of ministry needs to be intentionally practiced in today's church. As soon as a person takes over a position, chairs a committee, or starts up a new program, this leader should begin the process of mentoring other people to do the tasks of that position, serve as chair, or run the program after the founder moves on.

— Evaluation Exercise —

HOW CODEPENDENT AM I?

1) I (often, sometimes, never) see myself as responsible for some-one else's thoughts, feelings, or choices.

2) I (often, sometimes, never) have difficulty receiving help or hav-ing my needs met by others.

3) I (often, sometimes, never) get angry because others don't appre-ciate what I do for them.

4) I (often, sometimes, never) have difficulty knowing what I am feeling, even though I am very much aware of how other people feel.

5) I (often, sometimes, never) have a hard time saying "no" when people ask me to do things.

6) I (often, sometimes, never) do things in hopes that it will make people like me.

7) I (often, sometimes, never) feel responsible for keeping someone else sober, sane, or from becoming abusive.

For each "often," score three points. For each "sometimes," score one point. For each "never" score 0 points. Many codependents will score a perfect twenty-one. Does it surprise you that some people score very low on this test?

CHAPTER THREE

The Truth about Work Addiction

"I worked harder than all of them . . . "

The Apostle Paul, First Corinthians 15:10

A certain young pastor came to Jesus and said, "Lord, I already know how to be saved. What I need to know is how to move on from this parish and find the situation that I really deserve." And Jesus said, "Why do you call me Lord? I am not your bishop. Have you filed your statistical reports? Does your church pay all of its denominational askings, and have you organized every committee according to the rules you have received? Have you gone to all the workshops, visited all of the shut-ins, and said the invocation at the rotary each month?" "All these I have done," the young man said. "What do I still lack?" Jesus answered, "If you want to be perfect, go, love your family. Take the time that you need to establish your own spiritual disciplines. Guard your health, both emotional and

physical, and set reasonable boundaries for your work-
load. Give up on your ambition to meet everyone's
expectations for you will never satisfy them. Forget
multi-tasking and time management. Instead, simply
follow me each moment each day, for tomorrow will
take care of itself." The young pastor walked away dis-
mayed and sad for he was very ambitious and addicted
to mastering his job.

Immediately after the incident paraphrased above, Peter asks Jesus a
question, "Since we apostles have left everything, what will be our
reward?" (Matthew 19:27). Jesus assures the disciples that God will not
forget those who make sacrifices, but then he adds a "but." He says,
"But, many who are first will be last" (Matthew 19:30). Jesus then goes
on to tell one of the most difficult parables in the Bible. It is his story
about workmen being hired at different hours of a day and how those
who show up just for one easy hour of labor are paid the same as those
who were ambitious and able to work a full day in the hot sun (Matthew
20:1-16). This important story, the last that Jesus tells during the working part of his itinerant ministry, is largely ignored in the church today.
It's not that we find it difficult to understand, but that it contradicts
what we assume to be Jesus' message. We assume Jesus to be supporting
us when we tell our children that if they work hard and put in more
hours than anyone else, life will reward them. We say, "The early bird
catches the worm," but that's not what Jesus says. Not only are those who
work more hours not rewarded, they are sent home to their families
without any homework or opportunity for overtime. When one looks at
the whole of Jesus' teachings, one has to note that he is radically counter-
cultural, not only because he shifts religious merit away from
works-righteousness, which places an emphasis on what one does, but
also because he consistently rebukes ambition and is willing to challenge
as a form of idolatry the love we have of our jobs. He calls us to drop
our nets (the symbols of our workplace) and follow. His message begins
by telling us about states of being (not doing) that are blessed (Matthew
5:1-15) and leads us toward the grace of accepting his completed work

upon the cross. We must be careful not to let any attitude we have about our work, whether it be volunteer or paid, supersede our simple relationship to God through the gift of faith.

The way we relate to work is usually more of a problem than the amount of work we are given to do. Our attitude about work sets us up for burnout in three ways:

First, we are set up for burnout by our acceptance of the cultural myth that ambition and hard work will always be rewarded. When we work hard in the church and find that we receive neither the pay that others with the same qualifications receive in the secular world, nor the appreciation from others that we need, we get burned-out. Half of our mind tells us that we should be rewarded in an expected way. The other half of our mind tells us to keep doing our job because it's the "Christian" thing to do. As mentioned before, the state of being of two minds is inherently exhausting. The full weight of disillusionment will eventually collapse our ambition and cause us to become half-hearted, even though we may continue to work harder than anyone else (or at least we will feel that we do).

Jesus counters this attitude by telling us our service will be rewarded not for its ambition, but for its faithfulness. If we serve in the church out of faithfulness to Christ, we will find many rewards and momentary blessings. What drives true disciples of Christ is not pride in their being able to work harder than anyone else, but primary relationships. Instead of seeking reward for what we do, we find delight in our relationship with Christ, our families, and our congregation, which may express itself sometimes in periods of strenuous labor and at other times in periods of intentional rest and reflection.

Second, our tendency to worship our work and give it more importance than it deserves can cause us to ignore our body and soul's need for rest and recreation, as well as our family's need for us to be present with them. Jesus reminds us that the Sabbath was initiated and made one of the ten commandments to serve our human needs (Mark 2:27). Knitted into our design as creatures is a need for a period of quiet and sleep each day and a need for a day of recreation and freedom from labor each week. While the effects of not keeping a Sabbath each week may not be as immediately apparent as the effects of sleep deprivation, they are just as damaging to our health and emotional stability.

Jesus calls us not to be legalistic about our keeping of this needed time off. Instead, we should use it for the healing of our souls. Because we remember the arguments he had with the Pharisees of his day, and the way some fundamentalist traditions today seem very strict about what they will not do on Sunday, many of us are conflicted and confused about what habits we should form. Deciding appropriate rituals for honoring a day each week, particularly if one has to work on Sunday as most clergy do, is an important task in spiritual development and in maintaining a healthy marriage and personal friendships.

Third, we often look to work to give our lives meaning and to make us feel good. Since work can provide a high, and stress can generate endorphin, work easily becomes an addiction. It is hard for us to see work addiction as being as dangerous to our health and soul as its cousins, greed and substance abuse. Like gambling, pornography, and certain other compulsive behaviors, work is a drug that uses the brain's self-medicating properties to hook us into going beyond what is reasonable. Like any addiction, many of us who have been addicted to work have been led down a spiral of more and more irrational behavior until we have hit bottom. We recognize our own burnout, saying, "Hello my name is Bill and I am a workaholic."

Loving the Gift, Rather than the Giver

The Bible speaks about work as a gift, especially in this passage from Ecclesiastes:

> I have seen the burden God has laid on men. He has made everything beautiful in its time. He has also set eternity in the hearts of men; yet they cannot fathom what God has done from beginning to end. I know that there is nothing better for men than to be happy and do good while they live. That everyone may eat and drink, and find satisfaction in all his toil this is the gift of God
> (Ecclesiastes 3:10-13).

The fact that work will be challenging and often exhausting is understood throughout scripture as a consequence of humanity's fall into sin (Genesis 3:17-19). The fact that a job is difficult, important, and appears to reward additional effort, is not an excuse for allowing it to escape its appropriate space in our lives. Every good thing comes with boundaries. A farmer will not be successful if she allows her cows to graze in the cornfield, nor will we be successful if we allow our work to leak over into the areas of our live reserved for other things. Burnout is not only a consequence of inappropriate work habits, it is the warning bell that our whole life may lack the boundaries we need to be healthy or happy.

We constantly fall into the trap of paying attention to form and ignoring substance in the church. We focus on how worship is done and all its details, and forget its substance, which is the praise of God. We will also focus on the role we play in the church and forget the nature of ministry as a simple calling to follow Jesus. We receive our work, which is a gift to be used within certain boundaries, and we make an idol of it and worship it rather than our creator (Romans 1:25).

REINING IN AMBITION

The warning, "many who are first will be last" (Matthew 19:30), is one of the countless places where Jesus presents his vision of the heavenly kingdom as a radical reversal of things on earth. In the kingdom of God, the poor become rich, the oppressed go free, and the broken are made whole. Further, those who have achieved great things on earth are not necessarily given a great position in heaven. If we, like Peter in the above passage, hope working long hours and making great sacrifices will put us in heaven's penthouse suite, then we are in for a rude awakening, for the first will be last. We have no way of knowing how our particular actions will be rewarded or honored in heaven (see Luke 22:24-27). God may (in fact, Jesus implies this) recognize volunteers, part-timers, and laity as the most faithful servants. Those who have sacrificed and given 110% to the church may, in the end, be the least in the kingdom of God.

Jesus' story of the Good Samaritan is remarkable to consider in this regard (Luke 10:30-37). Jesus begins this story with a reminder that the innocent do suffer. A man, through no fault of his own, encounters bandits. There are congregations and mission agencies today who, like the Good Samaritan, seek to alleviate the suffering of others. If the culture of a church is rooted in compassion, the volunteers and staff rarely experience burnout in their work. Most congregations, however, have a missional mindset rooted in guilt and in keeping up appearances. Their workers are less likely to experience the simple joy of making a difference in the life of a stranger. Since their volunteers and staff experience the genuine rewards of Christianity less frequently (remember the rat in the maze in chapter one), they are more vulnerable to burnout. Jesus tells this story about the actions of a Samaritan, not to guilt us into working harder, but to draw us into working more compassionately.

The villains of this story are—please don't miss this—church officials. They are a priest and a Levite who come upon the broken and hurting person in the road and choose to pass by on the other side. It is easy to make excuses for them by saying they were concerned about their own safety or they were under an obligation to remain ritually pure. The simplest explanation may be that, like us, they were busy. They had important work to do in the temple and they needed to get there. There have been various studies done showing how much our willingness to be compassionate drops when we are in a hurry or stressed out. We have all experienced going down a hallway and, because we are in our own world, failed to recognize a friend. As our level of involvement and focus on our work increases, the resources we have available for those in need diminishes. The stress of trying to keep the institution running makes it less likely that those outside the church will find us to be Christ-like.

The Good Samaritan is remarkable for his willingness to put the work of his travels aside and deal personally with the need he saw. We are told how he had with him the salve and the bandages and the extra coins for the man's lodging. In our lives, God gives us resources to share—time, talents, and acquired skills. We share some of these gifts at our workplace and exchanged them for our salary. However, a portion of our time, talents, and skills should still remain at our disposal for helping those we encounter on life's journey. If we allow our work addiction to rob us of all our energy and resources, then we will pass by countless opportunities to live our faith and share the goodness of God. Note also that this story ends without any hint of reward to the Samaritan for his sacrifice. Helping others is its own reward. To be a good neighbor is part of the integrity of life that God desires from each of us. This is a higher calling than the zealous commitment for Christian sacrifice one often sees modeled in church leadership. Rarely are Good Samaritan neighbors addicted to their jobs, nor are they the type of people who have a non-stop commitment to the church.

Finally, Luke places this story just before the famous story of Martha and Mary (Luke 10:38-42). The two stories balance each other in speaking of faith as both active and passive, much the same as the Letter of James balances the theology of Saint Paul. The many church people described in James are like Martha saying, "I have works that prove my faith, where as you (Mary) demonstrate your faith by sitting still and praying." Faith cannot exist apart from time devoted to prayer, study, and Sabbath rest, any more than faith can be real apart from good works (James 2:17-18). Jesus, by lifting up both restful reflection of Mary and the neighborly-ness of the Good Samaritan, attacks our obsession with work from both sides.

From the moment Jesus met Peter, he began to overthrow Peter's protestant work ethic. Peter and the guys were fishing at the time and they told Jesus, "We've worked hard all night and haven't caught anything" (Luke 5:5). Jesus proceeded to fill the boat with fish—without working! As they followed Jesus, they must have noticed that Jesus wasn't organizing this discipleship thing in a very business-like way. He didn't hand them a job description. He stated their terms of employment in a simple line: "Follow me." He didn't require them to keep track of their hours or to perform certain duties. At times it seemed the only reason they were there was to watch. Why do we expect our current discipleship in the church to require us to work sixty hours a week or to volunteer for three different committees?

Our way of working is killing us. Many church workers are succumbing to stress related illnesses. Many of us have been made to feel guilty about squandering time on personal health, recreation, community issues, and family affairs. In order to overcome personal burnout and instill these more healthy values, we will need a radical break from both the prevailing influence of our work addicted society and from certain commonly held misconceptions about what Jesus wanted from his church workers.

Discerning a Good Sabbath

Ecclesiastes 3:1 reminds us, "There is a time for everything, and a season for every activity under heaven." This is in contrast to our contemporary culture, which views time as something in terribly short supply and in need of constant management. To say that some significant portion of our lives has been given to us for the activities of rest, reflection, fun, recreational exercise, and restoring our primary relationships is to make a radical religious statement. It implies that to do something else with the time, even something perceived as important and good, such as church work, is to act contrary to God. It is even more daring to plan ones calendar and bow out of certain events in a church setting with this principle in mind. To remember the Sabbath by actually setting certain blocks of time apart is a foreign concept in most churches (Exodus 20:8).

I have come to think of Sabbath time as a group of rest cycles built into the rhythm of life, and if I want to live in harmony with the Holy Spirit, I need to prayerfully discern these times and then take responsible actions to set them apart. These times come at differing intervals:

- Each day has a mini-Sabbath in that there is a block of the morning I set apart for devotional reading, biblical studies, and prayer. A good daily Sabbath also involves an appreciation for my body's need for sleep and exercise.

- The most critical Sabbath needs to take place each week. Of course, there may be emergencies such as fire, flood, and childbirth that disrupt a week or two. But like any principled practice, it only takes about three missed Sabbaths to lapse into habitual non-observance. Sabbath, like stretching exercises, is meant to restore elasticity to our lives. The irony is the more we need Sabbath, the less willing we will be to commit to it. We know it will be painful for us to give up the seven-day weeks that we think we need for our jobs. To keep Sabbath, we must first abstain from that which is materially profitable (anything we get compensated for), and second, from that which our spirit considers work. Full-time homemakers will need to have frank discussions with their spouses about how they can enjoy a day of rest in the midst of their family. This means clergy and most church staff should carefully choose another day, other than Sunday, for their Sabbath. Each person must discern the rituals and outward notifications to others that will form a boundary around his or her holy day each week.

- Some type of mini-retreat or day out of town every four to six weeks also celebrates Sabbath time. I meet with a monthly covenant discipleship group, and while our initial connection with each other involved church work, I find that the prayer support I receive from the others is an important part of my burnout recovery. Currently, there is a secular holiday each month of the year and part of Sabbath keeping may be to actually set aside this time for recreation. I think it is significant that the failure to keep the monthly "new moon" rituals was condemned by the prophet Amos:

> *Hear this, you who trample the needy and do away with the poor of the land, saying, "When will the New Moon be over that we may sell grain, and the Sabbath be ended that we may market wheat?" (Amos 8:4-5a).*

- Sabbath also comes in the form of yearly vacations. I know pastors who go on mission trips for their vacations or use these days to catch up with continuing education. Not only are they often cheating their families and failing to restore their primary relationships by remaining church focused on these weeks, but they also deny themselves the restorative nature of Sabbath time. While on vacation and taking a Sabbath, I rediscover I have an identity that is separate from what I do. I am for this period not reverend, but simply myself.

• Finally, life provides us with wilderness times when we need to separate ourselves and rediscover where God is calling us now. Once we open ourselves to Sabbath, we begin to learn the lessons that change teaches.

What Is Our Qat?

Half a world away from the bustle of our American lifestyle is a country called Yemen. In this land, people rarely work thirty, let alone forty hours a week. It has one of the world's lowest per capita gross national product and highest illiteracy rate. Government social services are nil and armed bands roam the countryside. In the time of Christ, this land hosted one of the most advanced civilizations of the day, but now there is little to recommend it to the traveler. However, if you go there, you may be invited to participate in the daily ritual of chewing qat. Qat is a bush. The leaves when chewed produce a mild euphoria. Most of the adults of Yemen devote a great deal of time and resources obtaining and chewing qat. Since it doesn't disrupt mental functioning, few Yemenites consider it a drug. But visitors rarely return from that land without wondering how different Yemen would be without this socially accepted addiction.

In America, we frequently joke about how coffee, chocolate, and sugar are socially acceptable drugs. Few of us devote very much of our time and resources to meeting whatever dependency we have to these chemicals. There is, however, a drug that many of us have felt a compulsive connection to and have devoted time and resources to obtaining.

Like caffeine and alcohol, it is easily and legally purchased and its users are rarely chastised for their moderate abuse of this drug, even if it ruins their social life. This drug is work.

Work addiction is hard to define because it involves a behavior rather than a substance, it is socially acceptable, and it is generally believed to be a means to improve life. After marriages fall apart, or after people succumb to a stress-related illness, we often say, "Oh, look at Joe, he worked too hard." We rarely recognize that we are all part of a culture that encourages people to use work addictively. Further, people who develop compulsions about performing certain functions and controlling the completion of tasks find that the stress produces an adrenaline rush. Many people who work long hours are meeting both a chemical addiction, as well as escaping from the relational difficulties of their home life. Just as some people drink to forget their problems, other people stay long hours at work to avoid the complexities of family relationships.

The stress we experience in church work often produces a small adrenaline rush in our brains that many of us find stimulating. When we watch someone playing the role of Martha at a church potluck, we need to see that behind her "martyr face" and her self-pitying there is secret enjoyment. She would never admit this to herself, but adverting two major crises and doing four impossible feats before breakfast makes her feel alive. It is her drug. Stress induced adrenaline, however, is part of the body's "fight or flight" mechanism. The reward it gives in exhilaration, it chemically steals from the body's healing mechanisms and from our capacity to be mentally flexible and spiritually whole. People who chronically run in hyper-drive are flooding their internal organs with chemicals that are only intended to be experienced for short bursts. Sooner or later, weakness develops and there are no healing reserves to mend the body. In the physical body, this weak link may cause anything from ulcers, bowel problems, and heart problems, to cancer. Just as importantly, the mental, emotional, and spiritual centers of our psyches deplete their needed reserves and we have nothing to sustain us in our daily labor. We reach bottom and become aware that we are burned-out on our drug, work.

Further work addiction, and the awareness of the burnout it has caused, can lead to other addictions. When we become aware that work has taken hold of our lives in a drug-like way, we go through the same five stages (the one's Kübler-Ross identified in those who are terminally ill) of denial, anger, bargaining, depression, and acceptance (see introduction, page 24). Because we become good at denying the effect of work on our lives and oblivious to our emotional shift towards irritability, we are vulnerable to other addictionsin the first two stages. We choose not to notice that our alcohol consumption has gone from an occasional social drink to a daily ritual. Pornography or gambling may slip easily into our private time because our heighten skills of denial keep us from sensing their evil. However, when we reach the stages of bargaining and depression, the search for something to counter the overwhelming stress we have invited into our lives becomes urgent. Options we would not have considered previously are now on the table. In the church today, we have many people who use some type of drug or compulsive behavior to bring them down at night so that they can sleep, and then use another drug to get them up in the morning so that they can handle the twelve-hour day ahead. Work addicts often reach the point where they accept they need to do something about their workaholic behavior just as their rising addiction to another drug is beginning to cause difficulties in their church work. Part of the reason our society is so willing to promote work addiction is because other addictions get the blame for the damage initiated by this compulsion.

Not everyone who works hard, however, is a workaholic. There are many who play Martha-type roles in their families, churches, and communities who are not addicted to their work. For some, family circumstance necessitates hard work. They work hard and long, but they are always aware that the work is a means towards the end of providing basic necessities. They are aware of the cost of work in that it separates them from their "real life." They keep an internal balance sheet between the time they have to spend working and the time that remains free for meeting their emotional needs. They can verbalize the choices they have made this week to keep bread on the table. Not so for the people who are work-addicted. For them, life is a smorgasbord in which there are no clear boundaries between work and real life.

There are others who have made short-term choices to work hard for a season in order to start-up a business or to move into a new position. They are not workaholics, even though they may now be working sixty to seventy hours a week, because this stress time has boundaries around it. They still have a personal identity that is separate from their job and will return to a healthy lifestyle when the rush time is over.

I have been careful not to define work addiction in terms of hours per week. Our society may have some wisdom in setting the average at forty hours per week, and I would say from experience that the impairment of ones relationships and spiritual formation seems to begin at around fifty hours. Rather than focusing on numbers, it is important to note that there are two things that separate healthy people from those who are work addicted:

- Workaholics inflict pain upon those closest two them. Their children may not speak openly about it, but in time they recognize they were deprived the presence of loving father or mother in their critical years. Workaholics devalue the self-esteem of those married or related to them by making them know that they are worth less than the church work that they are competing with for the work addict's attention.

- Workaholics use work to emotionally shutdown. They become numb people, unable to speak about their feelings or to be motivated beyond work-related goals. They have mistaken their job for a life. This trait reminds us that work addiction is a psychological disorder, often requiring therapy for treatment.

Many workaholics are the children of workaholics. This is not just a matter of inheriting a strong "work ethic," it is an internalized response to the trauma of parental neglect. In this way, work addiction is similar to other addictions. Work addicts are usually perfection seekers, such as was outlined in the first chapter. Work addicts, because they are emotionally shutdown, move progressively towards chronic depression and have difficulty with anger management. Both depression and anger are natural mechanisms, endowed by our creator, to help us know when vital issues are being challenged.

Both in business and in the church, workaholics are precisely the kind of people we think we want to hire and nominate to many offices. The upside is that they will literally work themselves to death. The downside is they may have difficulty with anger or other emotional issues. When they burn out, they will be difficult to replace. Work addicted codependents are naturals at making their job look undoable so they can always feel needed. The long-term consequences of placing people who have any serious addiction in key positions are catastrophic. Congregations must learn how to hate the sin of work addiction while at same time intentionally value the workers for who they are as children of God.

WHAT TO DO

Each of the three aspects of workaholic behavior has its solution.

- Against our society's emphasis on ambition and pride in ones work, the church must cultivate relational and spiritual values. Recovering the teachings of Jesus, which focus on being over doing, is an essential task for Christian's today. Congregations and denominational structures must become serious about modeling Jesus' attitude in their practice and policies.

- Against the propensity of work-related activities to leak into personal time, we must reflect upon how to keep the Sabbath holy in our lives. Often the Personnel Committee (PPRC) in the congregation has to take the lead in publishing policies that state clearly an expectation for employees and clergy to take weekly, monthly, and yearly times away from their tasks and the church site.

- Against the addictive properties of work, we must become more aware of how the stress response works in our bodies and how we may need to question the values we learned in our families of origin. Seeking a solution to our addiction may require participation in therapy and support groups. Congregational leaders must become more aware of the costs and warning signs of all forms of addiction. We need to move our congregational systems towards contributing to the holistic health of our participants, rather than simply responding to the crisis initiated by the symptoms of burnout.

Leadership Lesson Four

Good Leaders Model a Healthy Lifestyle

When clergy fail to model a healthy
lifestyle, they communicate the message
that work is more important than life.
How do we preach the message that spirituality, family relationships, and personal
wholeness are worth taking time apart to
achieve in a society where it is assumed that
"time is money?" If we deny our basic
human needs for the sake of a job,
we show ourselves to be morally lax
when it comes to the Sabbath.

— Evaluation Exercise —

ARE YOU A WORKAHOLIC?

1. ____ Is the amount of time or attention you devote to work an underlying theme in the conflicts you have with your spouse, children, or significant friends?

2. ____ Are there nights you have difficulty sleeping because your thoughts are still at work?

3. ____ Do you handle work-related phone calls or emails at home, or do you take work-related papers home with you on your day off?

4. ____ Do you lack any hobbies, or do you no longer have time for the relaxing activities you once enjoyed?

5. ____ Are you afraid you would loose your personal identity if you lost your current church position?

6. ____ Have you failed to take all the vacation and personal days your church grants for your position?

7. ____ Have you lost, or are you in danger of losing, something of value because of high priority you place on church work? This loss may be a significant relationship, such as failing to develop the marriage you wished for or the relationship you wanted to have with your children. This loss may be your health or your ability to maintain your home the way that you wish.

8. ____ Have people become so dependent upon you that you are afraid to take a sick day or a personal holiday?

9. ____ Have you failed to publicize your regular day off? Are people unclear about the boundaries of your Sabbath? Have you failed to spell out the types of emergencies where it is okay for them to disturb you?

10. ____ Do you regularly spend more than three evenings a week at the church?

Answering "yes" to any of the above questions is a cause for concern. The over all question you must reflect upon is, has the love you have for the work become such a high priority in your life that you no longer enjoy the personal life you have outside of the church? Or to put it another way, where is your soul? If you devote more of yourself to your relationship with work than to your relationship with God, your loved ones, or your inner-self, then you need to seek help.

CHAPTER FOUR

Boundaries and Burnout

"Be well, do good work, keep in touch."

Garrison Keilor

You load sixteen tons, what do you get?
Another day older and deeper in debt.
Saint Peter don't you call me cause I can't go.
I owe my soul to the company store.

"Sixteen Tons" written by Merle Travis (1947)
and recorded by "Tennessee" Ernie Ford (1955)

When "Tennessee" Ernie Ford sings, "Saint Peter don't you call me cause I can't go . . . ," you hear the agony of a coal miner who can never load enough coal to meet the expectations life has laid upon him. Many of us are afraid to die because we have not yet done all the things we hope will somehow justify our existence. Ours is the religion of the undone. We take seriously the expectations of our spouse, our parents (even if they are no longer physically present), and our church, even when those expectations conflict with each other. Sometimes, one of the most helpful things a therapist or a good friend can do for us is to lead us to question if those expectations are justified. We cannot make our lives legitimate by making other people happy; the only real debt any of us have in this world is to live the life that God created us to live. I find great comfort in the word of the Quaker mystic, Thomas Kelly, "We cannot die on every cross, nor are we expected to."

This chapter will deal with how creating appropriate personal boundaries and cultivating the proper use of the word "no" can help us overcome burnout. These tools limit the energy we lose trying to meet the expectations of others and give us the freedom to spend our time living the life God created for us to live. I will argue that no one has a better idea of what God's personal call and claim is upon us than we do. If we permit the expectations of others to keep us constantly busy, we will never be able to act upon the deeper callings we sense when we prayerfully search out God's plan for our lives. It's interesting that Jesus' first miracle was preceded by a rather sharp rebuke of his mother for her having the wrong expectations of him (John 2:4).

I am convinced that the number one cause of burnout is not the unrealistic expectations others lay upon us, but is instead the expectations we take upon ourselves. Further, I do not agree with common assumption that people are burned-out by their job. Sometimes we work at tasks that are not right for us to do. Sometimes a poisonous atmosphere of perfectionism, manipulation, and unreasonable expectation taints the workplace. No matter what our position, however, the purpose of burnout is to bring us to awareness so that we can act. Forming boundaries, along with the tools we have already acquired for dealing with perfectionism, codependence, and work addiction, is one more example of how we gain spiritual power by becoming more self-aware.

Being Yourself, Doing Your Ministry

Perhaps the most important boundary we need to erect in our lives is around the area of giftedness. If we constantly work at tasks that are outside our natural abilities, we will not only be working harder than others doing the same job, but we will be receiving less of the internal rewards our psyche receives for doing a job well. If the task is a simple one, a person who is not gifted at a task may do the task, as well as a person who is, but the ungifted person will feel less valued and have less job satisfaction. This naturally leads to burnout, because our inner nature looks for rewards.

There are at least three ways God uniquely wires each of us as persons:

First, God provides us with a certain temperament, what we often think of as personality traits, such as introversion or extroversion, task orientation verses relationship orientation, detail verses big picture, etc. These traits determine our level of patience—and conversely our sense of internal satisfaction—with a task. Carl Jung, and later his students, Myers and Briggs, opened up our appreciation of these human qualities. Their research showed that we each seem to be born with a propensity to learn from and respond to our environment in a characteristic way. Trying to swim against the current of how we are wired is exhausting.

Second, we develop in life certain talents such as the ability to play the piano or fix a computer. As Christians, we receive from God spiritual gifts for the purpose of work in God's kingdom. These additional skills are sometimes linked to our natural talents and sometimes contrast what we were given at birth. Paul is amazed at how God took his lack of beauty and oratory skills and reversed these deficits by giving him the spiritual gifts to be an apostle (Galatians 4:13-15, First Corinthians 2:1-5). It is important to understand, however, that while talents and spiritual gifts can be developed or ignored, they cannot be created at will. To do what we are not gifted to do requires extra energy and often yields unsatisfactory results. Besides, our souls feel rewarded when we have the opportunity to use our natural talents and spiritual gifts. Like a duck taking to water, we each discover a joyful energy when work permits us to operate freely in our area of giftedness.

Third, we each feel drawn to address a certain area of need in the world. Some people are drawn by aesthetics and find themselves excited about fixing the places where the church and the neighborhood lacks beauty. Others are drawn to ministry with children, with the homeless, or to address social issues such as racism. When pastors arrive at a new appointment, they rarely find that the congregation values their personal passion. Eventually, they may inspire and draw others into their passion, but this tension between church and pastor is always in the background and should be recognized. The Holy Spirit draws the heartstrings of God's people in a variety of ways in order to staff and fund the varied missions of the church. We are not called to understand someone else's passion, but we are called to be sensitive to our own hearts and not to forsake our personal sense of mission. One of the factors that leads to burnout in lone or senior pastors involves their role as generalists. One has to be well self-differentiated to thrive while constantly supporting everybody else in their differing callings and ministries. In the race to encourage others to be all they can be, pastors can lose touch with their own calling. Because it is only natural to feel most rewarded for the things you accomplish in your own area of giftedness and passion, you may find church work becoming less rewarding as you spend more time supervising others. It is the "Peter Principle": The higher you go, the less time you find to fish in your own pond.

Congregations also have temperament, passion, and spiritual gifted-ness as a corporate body. I like to speak about each church as having its own personality. It is important for congregational leaders to learn what their particular church is passionate about and to accentuate that aspect of the church's activities. One church I know had a great passion for health related causes. They participated enthusiastically in the American Cancer society's annual "Relay for Life," as well as supported all com-munity fundraisers relating to health. Another church enjoyed doing lavish theatrical plays that involved nearly the whole congregation, while a third actively feed and sheltered the homeless. In each of these churches, the laity rarely complained about being over-stressed or burned-out when they did something related to their passion and corpo-rate giftedness.

Many churches now regularly use spiritual gift inventories as a way of encouraging lay people to become involved in the church work that suits them. (See *Equipped for Every Good Work*, Discipleship Resources, http://www.gbod.org/equipped/.) Just discovering one's gifts, temperament, and spiritual passion is not enough to alleviate burnout. As individuals, we must intentionally choose to say "no" to work that involves too much of our time doing that which we are not gifted to do. This does not mean we should never pitch in to help in these tasks. Everybody needs to take a turn washing dishes. Instead, we should guard our main talents and gifts to keep them the primary focus of our service. The congregation, on the other hand, needs to be willing to let drop those programs and activities that no one seems to feel led to lead. When the church manipulates people into keeping programs alive that should have been allowed to die, burnout results.

Chaos and Conflict

There is an old story about a farmer who was taking his chickens to market in the back of his pickup truck. Every few minutes the farmer would stop, take a two-by-four, and pound the chicken cages in the truck bed. The hitchhiker who was riding with him asked him what he was doing. The farmer replied, "I only have a half-ton truck, and I'm taking about a ton of chickens to market. I figure I have to keep half of them in the air at all times."

Some church leaders are like that farmer. They constantly drive the program life of the congregation beyond its limits. I jokingly say that some people have the spiritual gift of chaos. There are people in this world who just love to stir things up. One person I know has a restless intensity. You ask her a simple question and she will give you five answers, only three of them with any truth to them. There are some people who have a gift of sowing discontent and conflict wherever they go. Chaos and conflict generated by such people will have an exhausting effect upon the other church leaders who are trying to keep the congregation on a stable course. This being said, these people who cause such trouble are often the most creative and giving people in the church.

I have struggled in a variety of congregations with the problem of how to allow such people to contribute their creative gifts to the mix of the congregation, while at the same time limiting their disruptive influence. I have come to accept that I am responsible for drawing boundaries around my own sanity. Just as there is a firewall in my car between the passenger compartment and the engine, so also I may need to distance myself from those well-meaning people who constantly create chaos and conflict. Further, in the church we occasionally encounter people who need to be kept within limited roles. The more honest and clear the leadership of a congregation can be in speaking about such situations, especially with the individuals involved, the better.

THE GOLDFISH SPEAKS

When I was at the peak of my own personal burnout, I had in my church office a bowl with a goldfish in it. I named the fish Polonius, after the overly preachy character in Shakespeare's Hamlet who said:

> This above all: to thine own self be true,
> And it must follow, as the night the day,
> Thou cans't not be false to any man (Hamlet I, Scene 3).

There is a certain irony in that line, for poor Polonius gets killed in the third act while hiding behind a curtain. Polonius, after warning others to be true to themselves, loses his own life because Hamlet mistakes him for the king. Polonius is a comic foil, so busy in the affairs of others that he fails to understand his own role or offer any worthwhile advice on how to live life. In naming my goldfish Polonius, I was confessing my own sin. So much of church work can become mere meddling in the affairs of others. The only way to be effective in our ministry is to be true to ourselves. As long as we try to meet the expectations of others, we will never gain the insight into our own unique role, which is important to health and peace.

The four causes of burnout call us to frequent and honest self-examination. When we become aware that we are burned-out we need to undertake the serious work of recognizing our own tendencies towards perfectionism and codependence, modifying our relationship to work, and establishing firm boundaries around our primary relationship with God and our temperament, spiritual gifts, and passions. Self-examination and the formation of boundaries may be for us something we constantly advise others to do, but then fail to heed ourselves.

Clergy families often find themselves stressed by intrusions into their personal space and privacy. Pastors who live in church-provided housing are aware that their home life is acted out in something of a goldfish bowl. When people cross the line into our personal space, it is only natural that we expend emotional energy pushing them back. Sexual harassment and misconduct are blatant examples of boundaries crossed, but many clergy have experienced more subtle encounters, where we become uneasy with the intrusion someone makes into what we hold to be private. We need to give ourselves permission to be aware of our boundaries and express discomfort when we feel it.

Not only clergy, but also anyone who becomes involved in church life soon encounters a moment when he or she gives up some degree of privacy in order to fit in with the fellowship. If the church is healthy, new trust-based relationships nourish our faith. But when we have made ourselves too vulnerable too soon, or when we have compromised our boundaries to a fellowship of people who have their own unresolved issues, our spiritual energy takes a hit. There are times when the only way to be true to ourselves is to retreat to a form of relating where we feel less vulnerable. It is healthy to want to limit the amount of personal information we allow the fellowship to know. This is an important boundary to establish.

Beyond Behavior Modification

This book began by talking about lab rats and the nature of burnout as a condition of awareness. When we wake up to the fact that we haven't been receiving the expected rewards for our labors, we enter burnout. Getting back to health involves both changing our expectations and restoring the joyful sense of abundant rewards that Christian service once gave us. Often, we want to find a shortcut through burnout's uncomfortable period of self-learning. We would rather modify a few behaviors, like not staying quite as late at the office as we once did, quitting a particular committee, or joining an exercise class. We don't want to admit that dealing with burnout might require us to make a radical shift. We might need to learn how to say "no" for the first time in our Christian lives. We might have to stop doing what others expect us to do. We will need to take on those tasks that nurture our hopes and employ more fully the temperament and spiritual gifts God has set within us.

Congregational leaders may have picked up this book in hopes of uncovering a few quick tricks that would stem the hemorrhaging of volunteers from church programs and quickly refresh staff back to vitality. But like the other five books of the series, this book is based on the assumption that every congregation is a system. Preventing burnout involves modifying every aspect of the working culture of the church.

To summarize, we must:

- Accept that burnout awareness is good and support those who seek revitalization or look for alternative areas of service after many years in one job.

- Conquer our tendency to seek perfection. The church must instead emphasize God's amazing grace.

- Address codependency as the inappropriate set of behaviors it is. We and the other leaders of our congregation should know we are valued not because we are needed, but because we are children of God.

- Modify our work habits to include appropriate times for Sabbath. Our rest periods must include the time for physical exercise, spiritual reflection, and restoring our primary relationships.

- Establish flexible but firm boundaries around each individual. Guilt is not an acceptable tool for manipulating people into doing jobs in the church.

The bad news is recovery from burnout is more than the simple modification of a few behaviors. The good news is we do not have to become terminally burned-out, nor do we need to accept the current dropout rate of our leaders as the cost of doing business. We can relight the fire; we can rediscover the joy of serving the Lord.

Take Peter, for example. We see him burned-out in the last chapter of John, but later we see him leading the greatest revival in the history of the church. He stands on the balcony in Jerusalem, so filled with joy that people can see the fire of faith burning bright, through him. The story of Pentecost (Acts, chapter two) can be seen as God's willing response towards those who prayerfully looked to God for renewed passion in their church work.

When all is said and done, recovery from burnout is spiritual in nature. This is perhaps burnout's greatest irony: people drop out of the church because of what they feel it has done to them, even though they need spiritual renewal, which the church can provide. While doing church work, we may come to feel God forsaken. But God has not abandoned the church, and God still uses the church to renew people's hearts.

Leadership Lesson Five

Good Leaders Appreciate Diversity

Good leaders match people with the opportunity to serve where they are both gifted and have a passion to see results. Good leaders train themselves to be sensitive to the way different people are equipped to serve in different ways.

— Evaluation Exercise —

THE TASKS FOR OVERCOMING BURNOUT

Task One: Become aware of our current emotional, spiritual, and physical state. Are we:

- Healthy? Do we honor our personal needs and maintain an appropriate balance between our church work and our personal lives?

- Accepting of the rat race? Do we spend our days simply responding to the expectations of others?

- Experiencing burnout? Have we become aware that we can't keep going on as we have been?

- Terminally burned-out? Have we dropped out and need a radical rebirth to return to Christian service?

- On the road to renewal? Are we currently seeking the resources and finding the appropriate help to return to vitality?

Task Two: Become aware of the role perfection-seeking has played in our becoming burned-out. Have we honestly evaluated the cost of the following, and taken steps to reduce our perfectionist-driven behavior as it relates to:

- Rigidity and loss of humor?

- Procrastination?

- Unwillingness to try new things and resistance to change?

Task Three: Establish meaningful Sabbath time in your life as a counter measure to work addiction. What spiritual practices will you do and how much time off for rest will you take:

- Every Day _____
- Every Week _____
- Every Month _____
- Every Year _____

Are there any additional concerns relating to your current stage in life's journey?

Task Four: Establish appropriate boundaries around what you will and will not do. Have you:

- Reflected upon your personal temperament?

- Reflected upon your personal spiritual gifts?

- Reflected upon where you are most passionate about changing the world?

What boundaries are appropriate for you to draw to prevent those who spread chaos and conflict from ruining your peace?

Where do you sense God is calling you to make changes so that you can be happier and healthier?

Other Books by Bill Kemp

Each of the six books of the *Congregational Leaders Empowered for Change* series will focus on problems that can become woven into a congregation's very culture, and so need the coordinated work of many people to achieve change. The emphasis is upon cultivating a broad leadership base that is aware of the issues and of implementing systemic changes. These books provide a common language that both laity and clergy can use together when they talk about the things that influence the success of their congregation.

- *Ezekiel's Bones*, reveals how spiritual passion is the fuel that keeps a congregation active and excited about the faith it has to share with the world. Without spiritual passion, a church, no matter its size, will either crash and burn or become a hollow shell of its former glory. Just as the body is fueled by a nutritious diet, so a church is fueled by a healthy, passionate, spirituality.

- *Jonah's Whale*, discusses how to keep the congregation united behind a common vision. How do we get to where we are going unless we know where it is and what path we should take towards it?

- *Saul's Armor*, looks at facility issues, as well as the problem of creating a flexible and dynamic committee structure in your church so your administrative process supports (rather than hinders) programs.

- *David's Harp*, deals with preventing, managing, and transitioning out of conflict. Every pilot must communicate and respond to negative information in order avoid stormy weather and collisions with other planes. We tend to treat conflict as an unwelcome intruder, rather than a routine part of flying. This book helps church leaders not to panic, but to see God's purposes in stressful situations.

- *Jesus' New Command*, deals with how to unite the congregation into a strong faith community. Love is like oxygen, vital to the maintenance of church life. This book provides tools for building intimate small groups while encouraging the congregation to be welcoming to newcomers.

Holy Places, Small Spaces (Discipleship Resources, 2005) looks at how small-church fellowships are faring compared to other congregations. It addresses the critical clergy supply problem and charts the changes that must take place for there to be a hopeful future of survival and growth for these congregations.

The Church Transition Workbook (Discipleship Resources, 2004) describes a step-by-step process that will enable the church to get moving again after traumatic conflict or being "run over by change." It keeps laity and clergy on the same page, as the church redefines pastoral relationships. The book includes stories, practical tools, and activities that will help the church see its current reality and the possibilities for ministry.